1973

THE DYBBUK

THE DYBBUK

A Play in Four Acts

By

S. ANSKY

Translated from the Original Yiddish by
Henry G. Alsberg and Winifred Katzin

*Introduction by Gilbert W. Gabriel and a
Note on Chassidism by Chaim Zhitlowsky*

NEW YORK

LIVERIGHT

LIVERIGHT PAPERBOUND EDITION 1971

1.987654321

ISBN: 0-87140-065-0

LCC: 26-11435

N   O   T   E

INTRODUCTION

RENAN thought the *Song of Songs* a drama in five acts and epilogue. If so, it was the long play of ancient Israel. Only out of anguish, terror and corruption would the Jewish dramatists of centuries hence arise. Only the torn breast of a people scattered among strangers could suckle such playwriting as Ansky's. Only the ghetto could bear so proud a child of beauty and dark dread as "The Dybbuk."

Wiser and more learned men than I must explain to you the origins of the old Chassidic superstition of transmigrated souls—of spirits of the discontented dead which suddenly possess the bodies of the living. Frazer will carry you back to antiquity with hearth-tales of the sort. I have seen the famous account of the Rabbi of Nikolsburg, Moravia, who witnessed the driving of a demon out of a victim's flesh. I have read a Cracovian doctor's solemn treatise on the whence and wherefore of these beliefs in the errant, clamorous, rebellious soul. I have heard that old Jews still tell legends of the dybbukim throughout Eastern Europe, and that the little children's eyes still shine blackly with grief

5

on hearing them. The theme is immemorial, this threnody of pity and horror which only a pious, lonely people can wail at the brink of death.

But I am detailed, instead, to tell mainly of the bringing of this great folk-drama of Ansky's over into English, and of what power and appeal it must impart in order to have become—as it has become— the idol of a notoriously frivolous theater-public. Something, too, of the effect of it on its first audiences here, and of the fine playing it has had in The Neighborhood Playhouse. I can use an eye-witness's sureness on topics like these.

"The Dybbuk" must have been a difficult play to adapt; almost as difficult as to produce. A stilted word, an exaggerated wrench away from the softly clanking honesty of its Yiddish original, might have degraded the whole magnificence of its brooding mood. Like all works which fly straight for the sublime, it is imperiled by numberless invitations into the ridiculous. To have preserved its poetry, its vigor, its village simplicity, its authentic quaint-ness as well as its deep, pervading mysticism—that was a sum of many deft and loving labors. This presentation of "The Dybbuk" in English owes much to the work of Mr. Alsberg, who so successfully translated and adapted it for the Neighborhood production.

Nor, either, can even a printed edition of the play afford to forget a debt to David Vardi, the Russian

actor who had taken part in the extraordinary
Hebrew performances of it at the Habima Theater
in Moscow. Mr. Vardi brought to his direction of
it here such patience, fervor and familiarity with the
scene as turned rehearsals into rituals of understanding. This preface of mine will have done its share if
it can at all appreciably reconstruct for you certain
of the scenes, the pauses and terrific tableaux, which
Vardi lifted out of silence into singing ecstasy and
picturesqueness.

Witness the meeting of Channon and Leah in the
synagogue of the first act: the young student, with
his wasted, blazing face, his eyes stabbed with the
pain of his doom and wild dreaming, his lips still wet
with the sweetness of the old Biblical lovesong he
had just stopped chanting; the young girl, ripe,
lustrous, immobile, devoutly quiet . . . how laconic
the stage direction is which tells you merely that, on
seeing Channon, she "drops her eyelids and keeps her
eyes downcast in embarrassment." For there shim-
mers suddenly over this motionless, dumbly yearning
pair such thrilling pity, such rapturous, palpitant
loveliness as turn the caked earth and straw of the
little synagogue's floor into the drunken fragrance
of Isolde's garden; and the dim mysteries of scroll
and altar change for a short moment into the stars
and flaming flambeaux of a swooning night in Corn-
wall.

Or, again, the dance of the beggars at the wedding
festivities in the next act: how can the curt commands of the play proper summon up to you (unless
you have seen it and need only be reminded) the
strident, torturous strangeness of this milling of
flapping rags and scabby shanks?   These pinched,
grisly faces of the poor are almost death-heads mili-
tant among the sleek living.   Their dance is a rattle
of dry bones, their bicker a howl of Furies which
sweeps the sense clear for that horrible, mad-minded
incident so soon to come—the entrance of the dybbuk of Channon into the body of the bride.

Ansky accomplishes in this incident, perhaps, one
of the most confounding, powerfully eerie uses of the
supernatural the stage has ever seen.   The perambu-
lations of Hamlet's father's ghost could have pre-
sented no problem so impish and immediate as this of
the unseen, renegade soul which, before your un-
seeing eyes, takes refuge in the breast of the maiden.

Still more fearful in its mixture of the physical
and spiritual, the explicit and the mystic, is the scene
of the driving out of this dybbuk, this disobedient
and defiant atom of inhuman passion, from her
swollen, retching throat.   Here is no pale gentility
of allegory.   The intensity of a peasant folk-tale
turns the play's period of catastrophe actual, almost
brutish, nauseating.   Yet this violence never pulls
an instant away from the plane of poetic nobility,
from a world where little miscreant merchants and

curious, comical old professional prayermen are sucked up into spaces of infinite and eternal love. The very ending of the play becomes, thereby, a benison of tragic, blinding joy, every short, broken line of it pealing and magically vibrant. No *chorus mysticus* is needed to turn this finale ineffable. It is, in its humbler, weirder fashion, greater even than the close of "Faust."

Over all such fiery happenings as these presses the stern shadow of life as these self-isolated Jewish villagers must live it. Their heads are turned forever back to the City of David, their only hope is a memory of those wisemen, kings and wonder-workers whose far-flung seed they are. With a certain sly humor, with pity for their poverty, grief for their melancholy, pride in their pride, Ansky gives you his fine genre pictures of the race at large, and of these odd, broken-off bits of it whom fate has blown into a little cluster in the grieving dust of some outpost synagogue. The marrow of sanctimony is in these people's bones. Their lives move by religious rote, and all their emotions rise and sink in the wailing of the *minyens*. Their very lusts are consecrated to the dictates of the immaculated Talmud, and through their prattle rush demons Dante could not comprehend. So they plod, huddled, sorrowing, revering, toward the grave, toward that small pillow of earth which is earth of Jerusalem.

Whilst there whistles this legend of the two poor,

outcrying souls of lost young ones—whistles down, from the shining Upper Air, to blow through the beards of old patriarchs, to toss their strict ringlets . . . and to give a great love drama unto Israel.

GILBERT W. GABRIEL.

Thanks are due to Mr. Joseph Meyerovitch, but for whose persistent encouragement, "The Dybbuk" might never have been translated into English.

A NOTE ON CHASSIDISM

By Chaim Zhitlowsky

THE spiritual sphere in which "The Dybbuk" lives and has its being, is Chassidism. This was the last great religious movement in Jewry of Eastern Europe, before the liberating forces of modern education had begun to undermine the foundations of the older beliefs.

The ancient orthodox dogma had reigned supreme throughout the Jewish world until well into our own times with Poland as its chief stronghold. Compared with this orthodoxy, Chassidism appeared a progressive, revitalizing and even revolutionary impulse. It became the source of a multitude of new ideas, and the basis of a new philosophy and ethics, imparting fresh strength to old institutions, reinforcing national consciousness and national aspirations, clarifying religious and moral problems and lending a new character to the whole of Jewish life and psychology.

Pre-Chassidic Judaism was well on the way to becoming mummified. The study of the Talmud and its innumerable commentaries had absorbed the entire intellectual energies of its men of learning. The greatness of scholars consisted in their ability

11

to unravel Talmudic tangles, rather than in opening new horizons of thought.

Piety meant merely the fear-inspired observance of the countless things permitted and forbidden by the Law which concerned itself with the minutest details of daily life. The religious Jew of that period was like a hypochondriac living in constant terror lest he forget to take this medicine or that at the prescribed moment. A possible omission, "God forbid," of a prayer or ceremony filled him with apprehension.

An overstrung nervous condition was the inevitable result of such a state of mind, a gloomy consciousness of sin and guilt, which frequently passed over into a settled melancholy. This pessimism had its root less in the individual's personal distress, than in his despair of the salvation of the Jews as a whole, their liberation from the Golos.

God punished Israel for its great sins. His face is turned away from its prayers because they proceed from an unclean generation. The promised Messiah will not come until the generation is worthy of his coming; but not even in the darkest hour does the Jew doubt that the promise will be fulfilled. To do so would be to commit spiritual suicide. The pre-Chassidic Jew, however, sustained his belief without optimism. He could not look forward to the imminence of the Messiah with the joy of "a bride awaiting her destined bridegroom." Deep in his memory,

the débâcle of the last two great Messianic movements still rankled, that of Sabbatai Zevi, in Turkey,
and of Jacob Frank, in Poland. Both of these had
broken down after arousing the most ecstetic hopes
in the false Messiah's pretensions. And when both
Zevi and Frank, together with their closest disciples,
abandoned Judaism to embrace respectively Moham-
medanism and Christianity, the great mass of their
followers were plunged into despair.

The holy and mystic writings of the Kabala, which
were the source of the Messianic movements, now
became invested with sinister significance. They inspired a mystic fear. To meddle with them was to
court disaster.

Only a few of the elect might study the Kabala,
and these not before the age of thirty years. A few
managed to penetrate its mystery, protected by the
armor of their holy lives. They learned how to perform miracles with the help of the mysterious powers
of the supernatural world, and were known as saints.
Such a saint was called a Balshem. His sphere of
activity was limited, for the most part, to healing.
It would never have occurred to him to attempt anything more far-reaching, as, for example, daring to
summon the supernatural world to his aid in helping
the Jews as a people, or in an effort to invoke the
Messiah.

An impassable barrier divided the natural from the
supernatural world which, with its divine powers,

dominated and oppressed the other. These powers were beyond opposition, attack or influence, nor could the normal course of human events be altered by any appeal to them. None but a great saint could accomplish this miracle, but in the sinful condition of the world, where could so holy a saint be found? Only the will of an inscrutable God could determine his advent.

The one hope of immediate salvation lay in the faithful observance of all the minute rituals, and in the study of the holy Torah. None but scholars and intellectuals had the knowledge to fulfill these observances, so that the great mass of the people, the artisans and village dwellers who were comparatively illiterate, were obliged to remain in ignorance and sin. This accumulation of sin added still further to the race's burden of guilt, and retarded still further their ultimate liberation. Thus an intellectual caste arose, and side by side with it a caste of the prosperous and well-to-do, who maintained them. The poor and benighted masses, however, continued to bind the race to sin and exile.

Thus the clouds of sadness lowered darker and darker over the Jews. A few chosen spirits, filled with sorrow and pity for their people, often spent their whole lives in fasting and other ascetic practices, flagellation and "Golos abrichten," i.e., wearing a hair shirt and wandering through the world as beggars. Through their own sufferings they hoped to lighten the load of sin which rested upon the whole of Israel.

At last a ray of light pierced these heavy clouds. They were dispersed and torn apart by a spiritual whirlwind, to reveal once more the clear sky of joy and hope. The saint who accomplished this supreme miracle was a Balshem, Rabbi Israel, known to later generations as the "Basht."

He achieved his purpose by a peculiar interpretation of the pantheistic, or more properly, panentheistic, philosophy hidden in the Kabala. His youth was spent far from the dusty haunts of Talmudic study, wandering over the open Carpathian country, first, it may be, as an "abrichter von Golos" and later as a healer in search of medicinal herbs. He lived among the people, the simple village-dwellers, whom the intellectuals despised. Amidst the lovely mountain scenery, his soul became filled with an intense love for the "God-World," and a powerful Pantheistic worship. Nothing is evil, nothing contemptible, nothing accursed. All things in nature and in human experience long to return to and merge with the source of their being.

Thus, step by step, he arrived at a philosophy which, by uniting the worlds of the natural and supernatural, broke down the barriers which had hitherto divided them. With the disappearance of the barriers, disappeared also the belief that man was governed by irrevocable and immutable laws.

The Balshem taught that the older creed was merely an illusion of the senses and the result of rationalizing. We, ourselves, create these rigid laws. But if we could lose ourselves in the love of God, then our vision would become clearer, our reasoning more true, and the illusions under which we labor would vanish. We should then see the world as a single whole, a world peopled by mysterious forces whose nature we could understand. And, most illuminating of all, we should discover the truth that we are ourselves an integral part of this mystical world, collaborating with the supernatural. As the flame of our love of God rises higher and higher, the individual ego merges with it. The soul also ascends until it attains the plane upon which the mystic powers dwell, and so becomes part of them. Joy and happiness are its reward, and the ability to take its part in the active control of cosmic events.

The immediate effect of Chassidism was to end the caste-system above described. The unlettered found himself on a level with the greatest scholars, indeed even higher if he happened to possess greater purity of soul, and a more child-like love of God. The caste of the rich and prosperous also gave way before the new aristocracy of mysticism.

The fear of transgressing religious observances vanished. God looks to purity of heart in the first place, and cares little for external piety. Far from diminishing the importance of the laws, the Chassidim gave them greater signifiance than ever, but interpreted them all in the light of mystical philosophy. All their interpretations moved in one direction, towards "Dvekus," the longing to fuse the soul with the divine Source of the world. And if an individual, for one reason or another, committed a sin, he knew that God was a loving father and that true repentance and amends would cleanse his soul and raise it once more to the heights.

Even more radical was the effect of Chassidic teaching upon the national hope and the belief in a miraculous liberation from Exile. Jews ceased to despair. The Balshem taught that as more and more people released themselves through holy living from their illusory world, and attained the True World of mystic powers, so much the sooner would they become able to achieve the salvation of the Jewish people, then of the whole of mankind and finally of the cosmos.

Under Chassidism the books of the Kabala were divested of their terrors. It remained necessary to exercise caution in delving into them, and none but the pure and holy might venture to do so, and even then only for the sacred purpose of aiding others. The road to holiness, according to Chassidism, was through self-abnegation, and only thereby could the Kabalist defend himself against danger.

Jewish youth, then, instead of absorbing themselves in the intricacies of Talmudic casuistry, let

the stream of this occult time bear them along.
They plunged into the depths of Kabalistic theory,
which told how the entire world emanated from the
Infinite Fountain of Light, and how the beams of
this light pass through all the worlds, until they are
transformed into what we know as Nature.

The more courageous of the Chassidic youth pene-
trated even the "practical" Kabala without fear.
They learned how to combine the various names of
Divinity, by which combinations they believed they
could become part of and effective factors in the
mystic activities of the forces governing the worlds.
In the course of these practices, the Chassidim had
miraculous experiences, and enriched the life about
them with marvels.   Wonders of every kind were
everyday events in the entourage of a Chassidic
rabbi.   The eminent Reb Salomon of Lyady, whose
ministry covered the end of the eighteenth and the
beginning of the nineteenth centuries, used to relate
with a smile how, in the house of his master, the
Sage of Mezheritch, marvels "strewed the floor of
his room."

It seemed, in truth, as though the wall between
the natural and supernatural worlds had indeed been
removed, and both worlds merged into one.

In the new mystical atmosphere, the people
breathed freely once more, and the spiritual powers
of their beloved Rabbis and Saints filled them with

a sense of security. No longer did they labor under a weight of guilt; they ceased to feel like outcasts, and hope revived within them. There could now be intercession in their behalf and their condition was no longer beyond redemption. Though the coming of the Messiah seemed far from imminent, they did not despair. There was a reason for his tardiness, and the Saints knew the reason. They knew everything that was destined to happen, and if they allowed the course of destiny to proceed unchecked, then the people realized that the period of their suffering was being prolonged to the ultimate benefit of the universe.

Sorrow and despair, then, turned to joy. Indeed joy became the watchword of Chassidism. Joy in being Jews, for the race of Israel had a cosmic significance; joy in a God of lovingkindness, who directs all things for Good, and has blessed the mass of Israel with Loving Jews, as the Chassidic Rabbis were called, to lead the people along the ways of righteousness.

Gloom gave way to good cheer. Brandy, song and dance induced a mood of pious ecstasy.

There is no doubt that Chassidism exerted a powerful influence for democracy wherever it became established. Old caste distinctions between the learned and the ignorant, between the poor and the rich, vanished away. The meanest beggar might enter the most sumptuous room and lie with his muddy boots upon the sofa, and, without let or hindrance, order the rich man about, as though he were his own brother. It is not to be wondered at, therefore, that the new doctrine gained instant victory over the old order of things, and so rapidly became the most potent force in the lives of the Jews of Eastern Europe.

The new philosophy inspired by Chassidism was in later years to find its expression, under the influ- ence of science and rationalism, in Jewish revolu- tionary and nationalistic movements. It is not re- markable, therefore, that J. L. Peretz, philosopher anarchist, D. Pinsky, revolutionary social-democrat, and S. Ansky Rappaport, socialist-revolutionist, and author of "The Dybbuk," should have been the first to express the older Chassidism in modern Jew- ish literature.

It was Ansky's purpose to draw us a picture of life in a Chassidic community, a life hovering on the boundary between two worlds, the world of reality and the faith-created world of supernatural forces. This life, with all its richness of spirit, will be found depicted in the pages of "The Dybbuk." *

* The author of this note was a close friend of Ansky's, and saw "The Dybbuk" grow in Ansky's hands from the first fragmentary notes, to completion in its present form.

CAST OF CHARACTERS
(In order of appearance)

Scholars in the Synagogue

Three Batlonim

The Messenger

Meyer, *the Shamas (Beadle) of the Synagogue*

An Elderly Woman with Two Children

Channon, *a young scholar*

Chennoch, *a young scholar*

Leah, *daughter of Sender*

Frade, *her old nurse*

Gittel, *her companion*

Asher

Sender

A Wedding Guest

A Beggar Woman with a Child

A Lame Beggar

A Hunchback

Bassia, *another friend of Leah's*

Nachmon, *the bridegroom's father*

Rabbi Mendel, *of the bridegroom's party*

Menashe, *the bridegroom*

A Beggar Man on Crutches

A Blind Beggar

A Tall, Pale Beggar Woman

First Chassid

Second Chassid
Third Chassid
Rabbi Azrael, *the Rabbi of Miropol*
Michoel, *his attendant*
A Minyen
Rabbi Samson, *the City Rabbi*

Act I
In the Synagogue at Brainitz.

Act II
The Street between Sender's house and the Synagogue.

Act III
In the house of Rabbi Azrael of Miropol.

Act IV
Same as Act III.

THE DYBBUK

ACT I

Before the rise of the curtain, a low mysterious chanting is heard in the intense darkness, as if from far off.

Why, from highest height,
To deepest depth below,
Has the soul fallen?
Within itself, the Fall
Contains the Resurrection.

The curtain rises slowly, disclosing a wooden synagogue of venerable age, its time-blackened walls streaked as if with the tears of centuries. Two wooden rafters support the roof. From the center of the roof, directly above the bima,* *hangs an ancient brass chandelier. The table in the middle of the* bima *is covered with a dark cloth. High up in the center wall, small windows open into the women's gallery. A long bench is against*

---

* Pronounced bee'-ma—Tribune in centre of the synagogue, railed round with a gate on either side, where the Holy Scrolls are read.

25

this wall, and in front of it a wooden table, covered with books piled up in confusion. Two yellow candle-stumps set in small clay candlesticks are burning on the table, but their light is almost entirely obscured by the heaped-up volumes. Left of the bench is a small door leading into a prayer-cabinet. In the opposite corner, a closet filled with books. In the center of the wall on the right is the altar, with the Ark containing the holy scrolls. To the right of this, the Cantor's desk, upon which burns a thick memorial candle of wax. On either side of the altar, a window. A bench runs the entire length of the wall, and in front of it are several small book-rests. In the wall on the left is a large tile stove, with a bench beside it. In front of the bench, on a long table, are piled tomes. Water container with tap. Towel pushed through a ring in the wall. Wide door to the street, and beyond this a chest over which, in a niche, burns the Perpetual Light.

At a desk near the Cantor's, sits CHENNOCH, *absorbed in a book. Five or six students are at the table along the front wall, half-reclining in attitudes of great weariness; they are engaged in the study of the Talmud, and their voices rise in a low, dreamy chanting. Near the* bima MEYER *is busy sorting the small bags which contain prayer-shawls and phylacteries. At the table on the left,*

sit the three BATLONIM,* *chanting. Their atti-*
tudes and the expression of their faces betoken a
state of pious ecstasy. On the bench beside the
stove, the MESSENGER *is lying at full length, with*
his knapsack for a pillow. CHANNON, *at the chest*
containing the tomes, his hand resting upon its
upper ledge, stands lost in meditation.

It is evening. A mystic mood lies upon the
synagogue. Shadows lurk in the corners.

The FIRST *and* SECOND BATLONIM *finish the*
chant, "Why, from highest height," etc., and then
fall silent. There is a long pause. Wrapped in
dreams, all three BATLONIM *sit silently at the*
table.

FIRST BATLON

[*In a narrative manner.*]

Rabbi Dovidel of Talan, may his merits hover
over us, had a chair of gold which bore the inscription: David, King of Israel, who is living still.

[*Pause.*]

SECOND BATLON

[*In the same manner.*]

Rabbi Israel of Ruzhin, blessed be his memory,
kept royal state. An orchestra of four-and-twenty
musicians played to him as he sat at table, and when

---

* Pronounced bat'-lon, Pl: batlon'-im—Professional prayer-
man.

he drove abroad, it was behind a tandem of never less than six magnificent horses.

THIRD BATLON

[*Excitedly.*]

And it is told of Rabbi Schmool of Kaminka that he went in slippers of gold. [*Rapturously.*] *Golden* slippers.

THE MESSENGER

[*Rising, and sitting upright on his bench, begins to speak in a low, far-off voice.*]

The holy Rabbi Susi of Anipol was as poor as a beggar all his life long. Often he depended on alms for his existence. He wore a peasant's blouse with a rope for a belt. Yet his accomplishments were not inferior to those of the Rabbis of Talan and Ruzhin.

FIRST BATLON

[*Annoyed.*]

Nothing of the kind; excuse me, but you're breaking in on us without any idea of what we're really discussing. You don't suppose that when we talk of the greatness of the Talan and Ruzhin Rabbis, we mean their wealth, do you? As though there aren't plenty of men in the world whose riches make their importance! No, the point is that a deep and secret significance lies behind the golden chair and the orchestra of four-and-twenty musicians and the golden slippers.

THIRD BATLON

As though everyone doesn't know that!

SECOND BATLON

Everyone that isn't altogether blind, does. It is said that when the Rabbi of Apt first met the Sage of Ruzhin, he flung himself at the Sage's carriage-wheels to kiss them. And when asked the significance of that action, he shouted: "Fools! Can't you see that this is the chariot of the Lord Himself?"

THIRD BATLON

[*Enraptured.*]

Ay, ay, ay!

FIRST BATLON

Now the essence of the matter is this: The golden chair was no chair; the orchestra was no orchestra, and the horses no horses. They were merely the semblance of these things, a reflection, and their purpose was to provide a setting for greatness.

THE MESSENGER

True greatness needs no setting.

FIRST BATLON

You are mistaken. True greatness must have the setting which befits it.

SECOND BATLON

[*Shrugging his shoulders.*]

How can greatness and perfection such as theirs be measured at all?

FIRST BATLON

It is no matter for jesting. Did you ever hear the story of Rabbi Schmelke of Nikolsberg's whip? It's worth knowing. One day Rabbi Schmelke was called upon to settle a dispute between a poor man and a rich one who was on terms of friendship with the king and before whom, in consequence, everyone trembled. Rabbi Schmelke heard both sides of the case, and then gave his decision by which the poor man won. The rich man was furious and declared that he would not stand by the Rabbi's verdict. And the Rabbi calmly replied: "You shall do as I have said. When a Rabbi commands, his commands are obeyed." The rich man's anger increased and he began to shout: "I snap my fingers at you and your rabbinical authority." Thereupon Rabbi Schmelke drew himself up to his full height, and cried: "Do instantly as I have said, or I shall resort to my whip!" This drove the rich man into a frenzy of rage, and he began to overwhelm the Rabbi with terrible insults. Then the Rabbi, perfectly calm, opens a drawer in his table—just a little way—and what should jump out of it but the Original Serpent, which coils about the neck of the rich man.

Oh, oh, what a commotion follows! The rich man yells at the top of his voice, and throws himself into the most terrible contortions. "Rabbi! Rabbi! Forgive me! I'll do whatever you command—only call off your serpent." "Tell your children and your children's children to obey the Rabbi, and fear his whip," answered Rabbi Schmelke, and called the serpent off.

THIRD BATLON
Ha, ha, ha! There was a whip for you!
[*Pause.*]

SECOND BATLON
[*To* FIRST BATLON.]
You must have made a mistake, I think. The story couldn't have meant the Original Serpent. . . .

THIRD BATLON
Why . . . what . . .

SECOND BATLON
It's quite simple. Schmelke of Nikolsberg could not possibly have used the Original Serpent, for that was Satan himself, the enemy of God— (May he have mercy upon us!)
[*He spits.*]

THIRD BATLON
Rabbi Schmelke knew what he was about—no doubt of that.

FIRST BATLON

[*Insulted.*]

I don't know what you're talking about. The incident I've just told you, took place before a whole townful of people—dozens of them actually saw it with their own eyes. And here *you* come along and say it couldn't have happened. Just because you've got to have something to argue about, I suppose.

SECOND BATLON

Not at all. I only thought there couldn't be any spells or signs that the Serpent could be summoned by.

[*He spits.*]

MESSENGER

Only in one way can Satan be summoned, and that is by the utterance of the mighty double-name of God, the flame of which has power to weld together the loftiest mountain-crests and the deepest valleys below them.

[CHANNON *lifts his head and listens intently.*]

THIRD BATLON

[*Uneasily.*]

But isn't there danger in speaking that great name?

MESSENGER

[*Meditatively.*]

Danger? No. Only the heat of a too intense desire can cause the vessel to burst when the spark breaks into a flame.

FIRST BATLON

There's a wonder-worker in the village I come from. He's a terrific fellow, but he *can* work miracles. For instance, he can start a fire with one spell and put it out with another. He can see what's going on a hundred miles away. He can bring wine out of the wall by tapping it with his finger. And a great many other things besides. He told me himself that he knows spells that can create monsters and resurrect the dead. He can make himself invisible, too, and evoke evil spirits—even Satan himself. [*He spits.*] I have his own word for it.

CHANNON

[*Who has never moved from his place, but has listened attentively to all this discussion, now steps up to the table and gazes first into the face of the* MESSENGER, *then at the* FIRST BATLON. *In a dreamy, remote voice.*]

Where is he?

[*The* MESSENGER *returns* CHANNON's *gaze with equal intensity, and thereafter never takes his eyes off him.*]

FIRST BATLON

[*Astonished.*]
Who?

CHANNON

The wonder-worker.

FIRST BATLON

Where could he be but in my own village? That
is, if he's still alive.

CHANNON

Is it far?

FIRST BATLON

The village? Oh, very far. A long, long way
down into the marsh-lands of Polesia.

CHANNON

How far?

FIRST BATLON

A good month, if not more. [*Pause.*] What
makes you ask? Do you want to see him? [CHAN-
NON *does not answer.*] Krasny's the name of the
village. And the miracle-worker's name is Rabbi
Elchannon.

CHANNON

[*In astonishment—as if to himself.*]
Elchannon? . . . El Channon! . . . that means
the God of Channon.

FIRST BATLON

[*To the other batlonim.*]

And he's a *real* one, I promise you. Why, one day in broad daylight he showed, by means of a spell, that . . .

SECOND BATLON

[*Interrupting.*]

That'll do about such things. They aren't for this time of night, especially in a holy place. You may not mean it, but it might just happen that you'll pronounce some spell or make some sign yourself (God forbid), and then there'll be a disaster . . . Accidents like that (God forbid) have been known to happen before.

[CHANNON *goes slowly out, the others following him with their eyes. There is a pause.*]

MESSENGER

Who is that youth?

FIRST BATLON

Just a young student in the *yeshiva.**

[MEYER *closes the gates of the* bima *and crosses to the table.*]

SECOND BATLON

A vessel beyond price—an Elui.†

* A higher religious school.

† A scholar whose genius consists in his remarkable memory, and capacity for learning.

THIRD BATLON

A brain of steel. He has five hundred pages of the Talmud by heart, at his fingertips.

MESSENGER

Where is he from?

MEYER

Somewhere in Lithuania—in the *yeshiva* here, he was famous as their finest scholar. He was granted the degree of rabbi, and then, all of a sudden, he vanished. No more was heard of him for a whole year, and it was said that he was doing the great penance of the Golos.* When he returned—which was not long ago—he had changed entirely, and he has since been going about absorbed in deep meditation, from which nothing ever arouses him. He fasts from Sabbath to Sabbath and performs the holy ablutions continually. [*Whispering.*] There is a rumor that he is studying the Kabala.†

---

* The Exile of the Jews. According to religious tradition, the golos was imposed upon the race as a punishment. In the original Yiddish the "Penance of the golos" reads "Ab-richten golos." The penitent, by wearing a hair-shirt and performing other acts of mortification of the flesh, and wandering through the world as a beggar, hoped to assist in the redemption of the race by shortening the period of exile.

† System of Hebrew mysticism.

SECOND BATLON

[*Likewise.*]

It has spread to the city, too. He has already been asked to give charms, but he always refuses.

THIRD BATLON

Who knows who he is? One of the Great Ones, maybe. Who can tell? It would be dangerous most likely to spy on him.

[*Pause.*]

SECOND BATLON

[*Peacefully.*]

It's late—let's go to bed. [*To the* FIRST BATLON, *smiling.*] Pity your miracle-worker isn't here to tap us some wine out of the wall. I could do with a drop of brandy to cheer me up—I've not had a bite all day long.

FIRST BATLON

It's been practically a fast day for me, too. Since early morning prayers, a crust of oaten bread is the only thing I've had a chance to say grace over.

MEYER

[*Mysteriously, and in high glee.*]

Never mind—you just wait a bit, and very soon there'll be a deal of cheer going round. Sender's

been after a bridegroom for his daughter. Only let
him get the contract signed—it'll be a happy hour
for him when *that's* done—and he'll be good for a
grand spread.

SECOND BATLON

Bah! I don't believe he'll ever sign one. Three
times he's been to get a bridegroom. Either it's
the young man he doesn't like, or else the family
that's not aristocratic enough, or it's the dowry.
It's wicked to be as fastidious as all that.

MEYER

Sender has the right to pick and choose if he wants
to (may he be protected from the evil eye). He's
rich, and an aristocrat, and his only daughter has
grown up a good and beautiful girl.

THIRD BATLON

[*Ravished.*]
I love Sender. He's a true Miropol Chassid *—
there's some real spirit to *them*.

FIRST CHASSID

[*Coldly.*]
Yes—he's a good Chassid. There's no denying
that. But he might have done something very different with his only daughter.

* A Jewish sect.

THIRD BATLON
How do you mean?

FIRST BATLON
In the old days, when a man of wealth and fine family wanted a husband for his daughter, he didn't look for money or blue blood, but only for nobility of character. He went to the big *yeshiva* and gave the head a handsome gift to pick out for him the flower of the school for a son-in-law. Sender could have done this, too.

MESSENGER
He might even have found one in this *yeshiva* here.

FIRST BATLON
[*Surprised.*]
How do you know?

MESSENGER
I'm only supposing.

THIRD BATLON
[*Hastily.*]
Well, well—let's not gossip—particularly about one of our own people. Marriages are all pre-arranged by destiny, anyhow.

[*The street door is flung open, and an elderly Jewess hastens in, leading two small children.*]

ELDERLY WOMAN
[*Rushes to the altar with the children.*]

Aie! Aie! Lord of the earth, help me! Come, children—let us open the Ark and throw ourselves upon the holy scrolls and not leave them until our tears have won your mother back from the valley of the shadow. [*She wrenches open the doors of the Ark and buries her head amongst the scrolls, intoning a wailing chant.*] God of Abraham, Isaac and Jacob, look down upon my misery. Look down upon the grief of these little ones, and do not take their mother away from the world, in the years of her youth. Holy Scrolls! Do *you* intercede for the forlorn widow. Holy scrolls, beloved Mothers of Israel, go to the Almighty and beseech Him that He shall not uproot the lovely sapling, nor cast the young dove out of its nest, nor tear the gentle lamb away from the meadow. [*Hysterically.*] I will pull down the worlds—I will tear the heavens apart—but from here I will not go until they give back to me the one who is the crown of my head.

MEYER
[*Crosses to her and speaks to her calmly.*]

Hannah Esther—wouldn't you like to have a *minyen* * sit down and say the psalms for you?

ELDERLY WOMAN
[*Withdraws from the altar and looks at* MEYER *at first uncomprehendingly. Then she begins to speak in agitation.*]

Yes—a *minyen* for psalms. But hurry—hurry—every second is precious. For two days already, God help her, she's been lying there without speaking, fighting with death.

MEYER

I'll have them sit down this minute. [*In the voice of a beggar.*] But you'll have to give them something for their trouble, poor things.

ELDERLY WOMAN
[*Searching in her pocket.*]

Here's ten kopeks—but see they say the psalms for it.

MEYER

Ten kopeks . . . one kopek each . . . little enough, that is!

ELDERLY WOMAN
[*Not hearing.*]

Come, children, let us run along to the other prayer-houses. [*Hurries out with the children.*]

* Ten or more adult males constituting a Jewish community.

MESSENGER

[*To* THIRD BATLON.]

This morning a woman came to the Ark for her daughter, who had been in the throes of labor for two days and had not yet given birth. And here comes another for hers, who has been wrestling for two days with death.

THIRD BATLON

Well, what of it?

MESSENGER

[*Deep in thought.*]

When the soul of a human being not yet dead is about to enter a body not yet born, a struggle takes place. If the sick one dies, the child is born—if the sick one recovers, a child is born dead.

FIRST BATLON

[*Surprised.*]

Ei, ei, ei! The blindness of people! Things happen all round them, but they have no eyes to see them with.

MEYER

[*At the table.*]

See, here's a treat from above! Let's get the psalms over, then we'll have a drop of something. And the Lord will have mercy on the sick woman and send her a quick recovery.

FIRST BATLON

[*To the scholars sitting around the big table, half asleep.*]

Who wants to say psalms, boys? There's a bit of oat bread for everyone that does. [*The scholars get up.*] Let's go in there.

[*The three* BATLONIM, MEYER *and the scholars, except* CHENNOCH, *pass into the adjoining prayer-room, whence the chanting of "Blessed be the man" presently emerges. The* MESSENGER *remains throughout beside the small table, immovable. His eyes never leave the Ark. There is a long pause. Then* CHANNON *comes in.*]

CHANNON

[*Very weary, walks aimlessly across to the Ark, sunk in meditation. He seems surprised to find it open.*]

Open? Who can have opened it? For whom has it opened in the middle of the night? [*He looks in.*] The scrolls of the Law . . . there they stand like comrades, shoulder to shoulder, so calm . . . so silent. All secrets and symbols hidden in them. And all miracles—from the six days of creation, unto the end of all the generations of men. Yet how hard it is to wrest one secret or one symbol from them— how hard! [*He counts the scrolls.*] One, two, three, four, five, six, seven, eight, nine. That makes

the word Truth, according to the Minor system. In
each scroll there are four Trees of Life.* There
again it comes—thirty-six. Not an hour passes but
this number faces me in one manner or another. I
do not know the meaning of it, but I have the in-
tuition that within it lies the whole essence of the
matter. . . . Thirty-six is Leah. Three times
thirty-six is Channon. . . . Le-ah—that makes
Le-ha, which means Not God . . . not through
God . . . [*He shudders.*] A terrible thought
. . . and yet it draws me nearer . . . and
nearer. . . .

CHENNOCH

[*Looks up from his book, attentively at* CHAN-
NON.]

Channon! You go about dreaming all the time.

CHANNON

[*Moves away from the Ark, and slowly approaches* CHENNOCH, *standing before him,
lost in thought.*]

Nothing—nothing but secrets and symbols—and
the right path is not to be found. [*Short pause.*]
Krasny is the name of the village . . . and the
miracle-man's name is Rabbi Elchannon . . .

CHENNOCH

What's that you're saying?

* The handles at the top and bottom of each scroll.

CHANNON

[*As if waking out of a trance.*]
I? Nothing. I was only thinking.

CHENNOCH

[*Shaking his head.*]
You've been meddling with the Kabala, Channon.
Ever since you came back, you haven't had a book
in your hand.

CHANNON

[*Not understanding.*]
Not had a book in my hand? What book do you
mean?

CHENNOCH

The Talmud of course—the Laws. You know
very well . . .

CHANNON

[*Still in his dreams.*]
Talmud? The Laws? Never had them in my
hand? The Talmud is cold and dry . . . so are the
Laws. [*Comes to himself suddenly. He speaks with
animation.*] Under the earth's surface, Chennoch,
there is a world exactly the same as ours upon it,
with fields and forests, seas and deserts, cities and
villages. Storms rage over the deserts and over the
seas upon which sail great ships. And over the dense
forests, reverberating with the roll of thunder, eternal fear holds sway. Only in the absence of one
thing does that world differ from ours. There is no

sky, from which the sun pours down its burning heat and bolts of fire fall. . . . So it is with the Talmud. It is deep and glorious and vast. But it chains you to the earth—it forbids you to attempt the heights. [*With enthusiasm.*] But the Kabala, the Kabala tears your soul away from earth and lifts you to the realms of the highest heights. Spreads all the heavens out before your eyes, and leads direct to Pardes,* reaches out in the infinite, and raises a corner of the great curtain itself. [*Collapses.*] My heart turns faint—I have no strength. . . .

CHENNOCH

[*Solemnly.*]

That is all true. But you forget that those ecstatic flights into the upper regions are fraught with the utmost peril, for it is there that you are likely to come to grief and hurl yourself into the deepest pit below. The Talmud raises the soul toward the heights by slow degrees, but keeps guard over it like a faithful sentinel, who neither sleeps nor dreams. The Talmud clothes the soul with an armor of steel and keeps it ever on the strait path so that it stray neither to the right nor to the left. But the Kabala. . . . Remember what the Talmud says: [*He chants the following in the manner of Talmudic recitation.*] Four reached Pardes. Ben Azzai, Ben Zoma, Acher and Rabbi Akiva. Ben

* Paradise.

Azzai looked within and died. Ben Zoma looked within and lost his reason. Acher renounced the fundamentals of all belief. Rabbi Akiva alone went in and came out again unscathed.

CHANNON

Don't try to frighten me with them. We don't know how they went, nor with what. They may have failed because they went to look and not to offer themselves as a sacrifice. But others went after them—that we know. Holy Ari and the Holy Balshem.* They did not fail.

CHENNOCH

Are you comparing yourself to them?

CHANNON

To nobody. I go my own way.

CHENNOCH

What sort of way is that?

CHANNON

You wouldn't understand.

CHENNOCH

I wish to and I will. My soul, too, is drawn toward the high planes.

* The founder of the Chassidic sect, known as the Basht.

CHANNON

[*After a moment's reflection.*]

The service of our holy men consists in cleansing human souls, tearing away the sin that clings to them and raising them to the shining source whence they come. Their work is very difficult because sin is ever lurking at the door. No sooner is one soul cleansed than another comes in its place, more sin-corroded still. No sooner is one generation brought to repentance than the next one appears, more stiff-necked than the last. And as each generation grows weaker, its sins become stronger, and the holy men fewer and fewer.

CHENNOCH

Then, according to your philosophy, what ought to be done?

CHANNON

[*Quietly, but with absolute conviction.*]

There is no need to wage war on sin. All that is necessary is to burn it away, as the goldsmith refines gold in his powerful flame; as the farmer winnows the grain from the chaff. So must sin be refined of its uncleanness, until only its holiness remains.

CHENNOCH

[*Astonished.*]

Holiness in sin? How do you make that out?

CHANNON

Everything created by God contains a spark of holiness.

CHENNOCH

Sin was not created by God but by Satan.

CHANNON

And who created Satan? God. Since he is the antithesis of God, he is an aspect of God, and therefore must contain also a germ of holiness.

CHENNOCH

[*Crushed.*]

Holiness in Satan? I can't . . . I don't understand. . . . Let me think. . . .

[*His head sinks into his hands, propped up by both elbows on the desk. There is a pause.*]

CHANNON

[*Stands beside him and in a trembling voice, bending down to reach his ear.*]

Which sin is the strongest of all? Which one is the hardest to conquer? The sin of lust for a woman, isn't it?

CHENNOCH

[*Without raising his head.*]

Yes.

CHANNON

And when you have cleansed this sin in a powerful flame, then this greatest uncleanness becomes the greatest holiness. It becomes "The Song of Songs." [*He holds his breath.*] The Song of Songs. [*Drawing himself up, he begins to chant in a voice which, though subdued, is charged with rapture.*] Behold thou art fair, my love. Thou hast dove's eyes within thy locks; thy hair is as a flock of goats that appear from Mount Gilead. Thy teeth are like a flock of sheep that are even shorn, which came up from the washing; whereof every one bear twins and none barren among them.

> [MEYER *comes out of the prayer-room. A gentle knocking is heard at the street door, which is pushed hesitatingly open, and* LEAH *enters. She has hold of* FRADE's *hand, and behind them comes* GITTEL. *They stop in the doorway.* MEYER *turns and sees them, and goes over to them, surprised, welcoming them obsequiously.*]

MEYER

Look! Here comes Sender's daughter, little Leah!

LEAH

[*Shyly.*]

You promised to show me the old embroidered curtains of the Ark—do you remember?

[CHANNON, *hearing her voice, abruptly interrupts his song, and stares at her with all his eyes. As long as she remains in the synagogue, he alternately gazes at her thus, and closes his eyes in ecstasy.*]

FRADE

Show her the curtains, Meyer—the old ones, and the most beautiful. Our dear Leah has said she will embroider a new one for the anniversary of her mother's death. She will work it with the purest gold upon the finest of velvet, just as they used to do in the olden days—little lions and eagles. And when it is hung over the Ark, her mother's pure spirit will rejoice in Eden.

[LEAH *looks timidly about her, and seeing* CHANNON, *lowers her eyes in embarrassment and keeps them so for the rest of the scene.*]

MEYER

Oh, with the greatest pleasure. Why not, why not indeed? I'll bring the oldest and most beautiful curtains to show her—at once, this very minute.

[*He goes to the chest near the street door and takes out the curtains.*]

GITTEL

[*Taking* LEAH's *hand.*]

Aren't you afraid to be in the synagogue at night, Leah?

LEAH

I've never been here at night before, except on the Days of the Holy Scrolls. But that's a feast day and everything is bright and joyful then. How sad it is now, though—how sad!

FRADE

Dear children—a synagogue *must* be sad. The dead come here at midnight to pray, and when they go they leave their sorrows behind them.

GITTEL

Don't talk about the dead, Granny. It frightens me.

FRADE

[*Not hearing her.*]
And each day at dawn, when the Almighty weeps for the destruction of the Holy Temple, His sacred tears fall in the synagogues. That is why the walls of all old synagogues look as if they have been wept over, and that is why it is forbidden to whitewash them and make them bright again. If you attempt to, they grow angry and throw their stones at you.

LEAH

How old it is—how old! It doesn't show so much from outside.

FRADE

Old it is, little daughter—very, very old. They even say it was found already built under the earth. Many a time this city has been destroyed, and many a time it has been laid in ashes. But this synagogue, never. Fire broke out once on the roof, but almost before it had begun to burn, innumerable doves came flocking down upon it and beat out the flames with their wings.

LEAH

[*Not hearing—speaking to herself.*]

How sad it is! How lovely! I feel that I want never to go away from it again. I wish I could put my arms around those ancient, tear-stained walls and ask them why they are so sorrowful, and so wrapped in dreams . . . so silent and so sad. I wish . . . I don't know what I wish. . . . But my heart is filled with tenderness and pity.

MEYER

[*Brings the curtains to the* bima, *and spreads one out to show.*]

This is the oldest of all—a good two hundred years or more. It is never used except on Passover.

GITTEL

[*Enraptured.*]

Leah, dear—just look. Isn't it **gorgeous**! Such stiff brown velvet, all embroidered in heavy gold.

Two lions holding the shield of David above their heads. And trees on either side, with doves in their branches. You can't get such velvet nowadays, nor such gold either.

LEAH

The curtain is sad, too—I love it also.
[*She smooths it out and kisses it.*]

GITTEL

[*Takes* LEAH'S *hand and whispers.*]
Look, Leah, dear! There's a student over there staring at you—so strangely!

LEAH

[*Keeping her eyes still more downcast.*]
That is Channon. He was a poor scholar, and he used to be a guest in our house.

GITTEL

It is as if he were calling to you with his eyes, he stares so. He would like to talk to you, but he is afraid to.

LEAH

I wish I knew why he is so pale and sad. He must surely have been ill.

GITTEL

He isn't sad really—his eyes are shining.

LEAH

They always are. He has wonderful eyes, and when he talks to me his breath comes short—and so does mine. It wouldn't be proper for a girl to talk to a strange young man.

FRADE

[*To* MEYER.]

Won't you let us kiss the holy scrolls? Surely! How could one be a guest in the house of God and leave without kissing His holy scrolls?

MEYER

By all means, by all means! Come!

[*He goes ahead, followed by* GITTEL *leading* FRADE, *and* LEAH *behind them.* MEYER *takes out a scroll and gives it to* FRADE *to kiss.*]

LEAH

[*Passing* CHANNON, *stops for a moment and says in a low voice.*]

Good evening, Channon. You have come back?

CHANNON

[*Scarcely able to speak for agitation.*]

Yes.

FRADE

Come, Leah, darling, kiss the holy scrolls. [LEAH *goes to the Ark.* MEYER *hands her a scroll, which*

*she takes in her arms and, pressing her lips against
it, kisses passionately.*] Now, now, child! That
will do. A holy scroll must not be kissed too long.
They are written in black fire upon white fire. [*In
sudden alarm.*] How late it is! How very late!
Come, children, let us hurry home—come quickly.

> [*They hasten out.* MEYER *closes the Ark and
> follows them.*]

CHANNON

> [*Stands for a while with closed eyes; then re-
> sumes his chanting of the "Song of Songs"
> where he left off.*]

Thy lips are like a thread of scarlet, and thy
speech is comely. Thy temples are like a piece of
pomegranate within thy locks.

CHENNOCH

> [*Raises his head and looks at* CHANNON.]

Channon, what are you singing? [CHANNON *stops
singing and looks at* CHENNOCH.] Your ear-locks
are wet. You have been to the Mikva * again.

CHANNON

Yes.

CHENNOCH

When you perform the ablutions, do you also use

* Ritual bath.

spells and go through all the ceremonies prescribed by the book of Roziel? *

CHANNON

Yes.

CHENNOCH

You aren't afraid to?

CHANNON

No.

CHENNOCH

And you fast from Sabbath to Sabbath—isn't that hard for you?

CHANNON

It's harder for me to eat on the Sabbath than to fast the whole week. [*Pause.*] I've lost all desire to eat.

CHENNOCH

[*Inviting confidence.*]

What do you do all this for? What do you expect to gain by it?

CHANNON

[*As if to himself.*]

I wish . . . I wish to attain possession of a clear and sparkling diamond, and melt it down in tears and inhale it into my soul. I want to attain to the rays of the third plane of beauty. I want . . .

* One of the books of the Kabala.

[*Suddenly in violent perturbation.*] Yes—there are still two barrels of golden pieces which I *must* get, for him who can count only gold pieces.

CHENNOCH

[*Appalled.*]
Channon, be careful! You're on a slippery road. No holy powers will help you to achieve these things.

CHANNON

[*Challenging him.*]
And if the *holy* powers will not, then?

CHENNOCH

[*Terrified.*]
I'm afraid to talk to you! I'm afraid to be near you!
[*He rushes out.* CHANNON *remains behind, his face full of defiance.* MEYER *comes back from the street.* The FIRST BATLON *emerges from the prayer-room.*]

FIRST BATLON

Eighteen psalms—that's enough and to spare! I suppose she doesn't expect to get the whole bookful for a kopek! You go and tell them, Meyer. Once they get started, there's no stopping them till they've said them all.
[*Enter* ASHER *in great excitement.*]

ASHER

I just met Baruch the tailor. He's come back from Klimovka—that's where Sender's been to meet the bridegroom's people. They haven't come to terms yet, it seems. Sender insisted that the bridegroom's father should board the couple for ten years, but he stood out for only five. So they all went back home again.

MEYER

That makes the fourth time.

FIRST BATLON

Heartbreaking, isn't it?

MESSENGER

[*To* THIRD BATLON, *smiling.*]
A little while ago you said yourself that all marriages were prearranged by destiny.

CHANNON

[*Straightening up and speaking in a voice of rapture.*]
I have won again.
[*He falls exhausted onto a bench, his face alight with joy.*]

MESSENGER

[*Taking a lantern out of his bag.*]
Time to get ready for the road again.

MEYER

What's your hurry?

MESSENGER

I'm a messenger. Great ones and magnates employ me to carry important communications and rare treasures for them. I am obliged to hurry— my time is not my own.

MEYER

You ought to wait until daybreak at least.

MESSENGER

That is still a long way off, and I have far to go. I shall start about midnight.

MEYER

It's pitch-dark outside.

MESSENGER

I shan't lose my way with this lantern.
   [*The scholars and* BATLONIM *come out of the prayer-room.*]

SECOND BATLON

Good luck be with us. May the Lord send the sick woman a complete recovery.

ALL

Amen.

FIRST BATLON

Now let's go and get ten kopeks' worth of cakes and brandy.

MEYER

It's here already. [*Takes a bottle and cakes from under his coat.*] Come on, let's drink a health!
　　[*The door opens and* SENDER *enters, coat unbuttoned, hat on the back of his head, thoroughly happy. Three or four men follow him in.*]

MEYER AND THE THREE BATLONIM

Oh, Reb Sender—welcome, welcome . . .

SENDER

Happened to be passing. I really must go in, says I to myself, and see what our people are doing. [*Noticing the bottle in* MEYER'S *hand.*] I'll surely find them studying, says I, or deep in pious discussions. And what do I see? They're all deep in preparing for a celebration instead! Ha, ha, ha! Typical Miropol Chassidim!

FIRST BATLON

Will you have a drop with us, Reb Sender?

SENDER

No, blockhead. I won't. I'll stand treat myself
—and splendid treat at that! Congratulate me—
this is a happy day for me. I have betrothed my
daughter.

[CHANNON, *distraught, rises from his bench.*]

ALL

Mazeltov! Mazeltov!*

MEYER

Somebody just told us you hadn't been able to
come to terms with the bridegroom's father, and so
it had all fallen through.

THIRD BATLON

We were heartbroken to hear it.

SENDER

It nearly did, but at the last moment he gave in,
and so the contract was signed. May good luck go
with it.

CHANNON

Betrothed? Betrothed? How can that be? [*In
despair.*] So it was all of no avail—neither the
fasts, nor the ablutions, nor the spells, nor the symbols. All in vain. . . . So what remains? What is

* Good luck.

there still to do . . . by what means . . . [*He clutches the breast of his kaftan, and his face is illuminated with ecstasy.*] Ah! The secret of the Double Name is revealed to me. Ah! I see him. I . . . I . . . I have won!

[*He falls to the ground.*]

MESSENGER

[*Opens his lantern.*]
The wick has burnt down. A new one must be lighted.

[*An ominous pause.*]

SENDER

Meyer, why is it so dark in here? Let's have some light.

[MEYER *lights another light.*]

MESSENGER

[*Crosses quietly to* SENDER.]
Did you come to terms with the bridegroom's father?

SENDER

[*Surprised, and somewhat frightened, looks at him.*]
I did.

MESSENGER

Sometimes it happens that the relatives promise,

and then go back on their word. And litigation follows. It pays to be very careful in these matters.

SENDER

[*In alarm.*]
Who is this man? I don't know him.

MEYER

He is not from these parts. He is a Messenger.

SENDER

What does he want of me?

MEYER

I don't know.

SENDER

[*More calmly.*]
Asher, run over to my house and ask them to pre-
pare some wine and preserves and something good
to eat. Hurry up, now—run along. [ASHER
hastens out.] We might as well stay here and talk a
bit while they're getting things ready. Hasn't one
of you some new parable of our Rabbi's? A saying,
or a miracle, or a proverb . . . each of his looks is
more precious than pearls.

FIRST BATLON

[*To* MEYER.]
Keep the bottle. It'll come in handy tomorrow.
[MEYER *puts it away.*]

MESSENGER

I'll tell you one of his proverbs. One day a Chassid came to the Rabbi—he was rich, but a miser. The Rabbi took him by the hand and led him to the window. "Look out there," he said. And the rich man looked into the street. "What do you see?" asked the Rabbi. "People," answers the rich man. Again the Rabbi takes him by the hand, and this time leads him to the mirror. "What do you see now?" he says. "Now I see myself," answers the rich man. Then the Rabbi says: "Behold—in the window there is glass and in the mirror there is glass. But the glass of the mirror is covered with a little silver, and no sooner is the silver added than you cease to see others but see only yourself."

THIRD BATLON

Oh, oh, oh! Sweeter than honey!

FIRST BATLON

Holy words!

SENDER

[*To the* MESSENGER.]
You are trying to score off me, eh?

MESSENGER

God forbid!

SECOND BATLON

Let's have a song!   [*To the* THIRD BATLON.]
Sing the Rabbi's tune.

> [*The* THIRD BATLON *begins intoning a low mysterious Chassidic tune in which the rest join.*]

SENDER

[*Rising.*]
And now a dance, a round dance. . . . Shall
Sender give away his only daughter, and not celebrate it with a round dance?   *Nice* Chassidim we'd
be!

> [SENDER, *the three* BATLONIM *and* MEYER *put
> their arms on one another's shoulders and
> start turning in a ring, their eyes dim with
> ecstasy, chanting a weird, monotonous air.
> They revolve slowly, on the same spot.   Then*
> SENDER *breaks away from the circle.*]

SENDER

Now a merry one.   Come on—all together!

SECOND BATLON

Yes, come on, boys—let's all join in!   [*Several of
the scholars join them.*]   Chennoch, Channon, where

are you? We're going to have a merry dance—
come on!

SENDER

[*Somewhat perturbed.*]

Ah, Channon . . . he's here, my little Channon,
isn't he? Where is he, eh? Bring him here—I want
him.

MEYER

[*Sees* CHANNON *on the floor.*]
He's asleep on the floor.

SENDER

Wake him up then. Wake him up.

MEYER

[*Tries to rouse him. Frightened.*]
I can't——

[*They all crowd round* CHANNON, *and try to
wake him.*]

FIRST BATLON

[*With a frightened cry.*]
He's dead.

THIRD BATLON

The book of Roziel, the King—look—it's fallen
out of his hand!

[*Consternation.*]

CURTAIN

ACT II

A square in Brainitz. Left, the old synagogue, built of wood and of ancient architecture. In front of it, somewhat to one side, a mound surmounted by a gravestone bearing the inscription, "Here lie a pure and holy bridegroom and bride, murdered to the glory of God in the year 5408. Peace be with them." An alley on one side of the synagogue, leading to a group of small houses which merge into the backdrop.

At the right, SENDER's house, also built of wood, but of imposing size and adorned with a balcony and stoop. Past the house a wide double-gate to the courtyard gives onto another alley with a row of small shops which also merge into the backdrop. On the drop to the right, past the shops, an inn, then the garden of a large estate and the owner's mansion. A wide road leading down to a river upon whose farther bank a cemetery is seen. To the left, a bridge over the river and a mill.

In the foreground, bathhouse and poorhouse. In the far distance, a forest. The double gates to SENDER's courtyard stand wide open. Long tables have been set out in the yard, and jut out onto the square. The tables are spread with food

68

which the poor, old and young, some of them crippled, are ravenously devouring. They are served continuously from the house, from great bowls of food and baskets with bread.

Before the shops and houses, women sit knitting, but their eyes hardly leave SENDER's house. Men, old and young, leave the synagogue carrying their prayer-shawls and phylacteries, and go into the shops and houses. Some stand about talking in groups. Music is heard from the courtyard. Then dancing and the confused sound of voices.

It is evening. In the middle of the street, in front of the synagogue stands the WEDDING GUEST, a middle-aged Jew in a satin kaftan, his hands stuck into his belt. The SECOND BATLON is with him.

GUEST

[*Gazing at the synagogue.*]

A great synagogue you have here—a handsome building indeed—and spacious, too. The spirit of God is upon it. Very old, I should say.

SECOND BATLON

Very old it is. Our ancients say that not even their grandfathers could remember when it was built.

GUEST

[*Seeing the grave.*]

And what is that? [*He reads the inscription.*]

"Here lie a pure and holy bridegroom and bride, murdered to the glory of God in the year 5408." A bride and bridegroom—murdered to the glory of God?

SECOND BATLON

Yes—by that bandit Chamilouk *—may his name be wiped out forever,—when he raided the city with his Cossacks and massacred half the Jews. He murdered that bride and groom as they were being led to the wedding canopy. They were buried on the very spot, in one grave together. Ever since, it has been called the holy grave. [*Whispering, as if he were telling a secret.*] At every marriage ceremony, the rabbi hears sighs from the grave, and it has become a time-honored custom for the people leaving the synagogue after a wedding to go and dance there, to cheer the dead bride and bridegroom where they lie.

GUEST

An excellent custom. . . .

MEYER

[*Coming out of SENDER's house.*]

Ah, such a feast for the poor. Never in all my born days have I seen the equal of this spread Sender's made for them.

* Chmelnitzki the Cossack chieftain who led a great uprising in which thousands of Jews perished.

GUEST

No wonder. He's giving away his only daughter.

MEYER

[*With enthusiasm.*]
First a piece of fish; then a cut of roast, and a zimmis * to top it off. And cake and brandy before the meal began! . . . It must have cost him a fortune—more than can ever be reckoned up!

SECOND BATLON

Leave it to Sender to know his own business. When it comes to skimping an invited guest, you know where you are—let him snort all he likes, he can't do anything. But it's flying in the face of danger not to treat the poor right. There's no telling who a beggar's coat may be hiding. A beggar maybe, but maybe also someone quite different . . . a nister † . . . or one of the Thirty-six.‡

MEYER

Why not the Prophet Elijah himself? He always appears as a beggar.

GUEST

It's not only the poor it pays to be careful with.

* A vegetable delicacy.
† A saint disguised.
‡ Thirty-Six men of virtue, on whose account God allows the world to continue.

You can't say for a certainty who any man might have been in his last existence, nor what he is doing on earth.

[*From the alley on the right, the* MESSENGER *enters, with his knapsack on his shoulder.*]

MEYER

[*To the* MESSENGER.]
Sholom aleichem *—you have come back, I see.

MESSENGER

I have been sent to you again.

MEYER

You have come in good season, in time for a great wedding.

MESSENGER

I know—it is the talk of all the country round.

MEYER

Did you happen to pass the bridegroom's party on the way? They are late.

MESSENGER

The bridegroom will arrive in good time.
[*He goes into the synagogue, and the* GUEST, MEYER *and the* SECOND BATLON *turn into*

* Peace be with you.

SENDER'S courtyard. LEAH appears beyond the tables, in her wedding-dress, dancing with one after another of the old women. The rest crowd about her. Those with whom she has finished dancing pass into the square, and stand talking in groups.]

A POOR WOMAN

[*With child holding on to her skirts. In a tone of satisfaction.*]
I danced with the bride.

LAME WOMAN

So did I. I took her round the waist and danced with her too. Hee, hee, hee!

A HUNCHBACK

How's that? The bride only dancing with the women? I'm going to take her by the waist myself, and swing her round and round. Ha, ha, ha!
[*General laughter among the beggars.*]

[*FRADE, GITTEL and BASSIA come from the house onto the stoop.*]

FRADE

[*Worried.*]
Oh, dear! Oh, dear! There's the darling still dancing with those people. She'll make herself dizzy

if she doesn't stop.   Go and tell her to come here, children.

GITTEL

[*Going to* LEAH.]

Come away, Leah dear—you've danced enough now.

BASSIA

Yes—you'll be getting dizzy. . . .

> [*They take* LEAH's *hands and try to draw her away.*]

THE POOR WOMEN

> [*Gather round* LEAH *beseeching her in whining tones.*]

She hasn't danced with *me* yet. . . . Aren't I as good as them? . . . I've been waiting an hour. . . . Me. . . Me. . . . It's my turn after Elka. . . . She's been round ten times and more with that lame Yachna, and not one single turn with me. . . . I've never got no luck!

> [MEYER *comes out into the square and stands on the bench. In a high-pitched voice, he chants the following verse in the manner of a herald.*]

Come in, come in, and feast your fill,
Rich Sender bids you straightway come!
Here's abundance and goodwill,
And ten kopeks for everyone!

THE POOR
[*Run out jostling one another.*]
Ten kopeks! Ten kopeks!
[*The square is left empty except for* LEAH,
GITTEL, BASSIA *and an old half-blind beggar
woman.*]

THE OLD WOMAN
[*Seizes* LEAH.]
I don't want no alms. . . . I only want you to
dance with me. Just once—just one turn. That's
all. I've not danced once these forty years. . . .
Oh, how I used to dance when *I* was a girl! How I
did dance! [LEAH *dances with her, but when she
tries to release herself, the crone will not let her go,
but begs for more and more.*] Again . . . again.
. . . [*They swing round faster still, the old woman
now out of breath and hysterical.*] More . . .
more. . . .

[GITTEL *has to force her into the courtyard.
Then she comes back, and together with* BAS-
SIA, *they assist* LEAH *to a bench.* SENDER'S
servants clear the tables and close the gate.]

FRADE
Oh, my darling, you're as white as a sheet.
They've worn you out, so they have.

LEAH

[*Sits with closed eyes, her head leaning back-ward, and when she speaks, it is as though in a trance.*]

They seized me . . . they kept on turning and turning round me . . . so close . . . and clutched me to them with their cold, withered hands . . . my head swam . . . my heart turned faint. Then some-one came and lifted me from the ground and carried me far away, very far away.

BASSIA

[*In great anxiety.*]

Oh, Leah, look how they've crushed your dress— it's all dirty now. Whatever will you do?

LEAH

[*In the same manner as before.*]

If the bride is left alone before the wedding, spirits come and carry her off.

FRADE

[*Alarmed.*]

What can have put such ideas into your head, my child? We may not mention the dark people—you know that. They're lurking in every tiny hole and corner and crevice. They see everything and hear everything—and they're forever on the alert to catch

their unclean names on our lips.   Then out they
spring on top of you.

[*She spits three times.*]

LEAH

[*Opens her eyes.*]
My spirits are not evil ones.

FRADE

Don't you believe them, my child.   The minute you
trust one of the dark people, he becomes unmanage-
able and begins to do mischief.

LEAH

[*With utter conviction.*]
Granny—it isn't evil spirits that surround us,
but souls of those who died before their time, and
come back again to see all that we do and hear all
that we say.

FRADE

God help you, child, what is the meaning of all
this?   Souls?   What souls?   The souls of the pure
and good fly up to heaven and stay there at rest in
the bright garden of Eden.

LEAH

No, granny—they are with us here.   [*Her tone
changes.*]   Grandmother, every one of us is born to

a long life of many, many years. If he die before
his years are done, what becomes of the life he has
not lived, do you think? What becomes of his joys
and sorrows, and all the thoughts he had not time to
think, and all the things he hadn't time to do?
Where are the children he did not live long enough
to bring into the world? Where does all that go to?
Where? [*Lost in thought, she continues.*] There
was a lad here, granny . . . his mind was full of
wisdom and his soul was set on holy purposes. Long
years stretched out before him. Then one day, without warning, his life is destroyed. And strangers
bury him in strange earth. [*Desperately.*] What
has become of the rest of him? His speech that
has been silenced? His prayers that have been cut
off? . . . Grandmother—when a candle blows out
we light it again and it goes on burning down to the
end. So how can a human life which goes out before
it has burnt down, remain put out forever? . . .
How can it, granny?

FRADE
[*Shaking her head.*]
Daughter, you must not think about such things.
He who lives above knows the reason for His actions.
We are blind and know nothing.

[*The MESSENGER approaches them unnoticed,
and remains standing close behind them.*]

LEAH

[*Not hearing her. With deep conviction.*]

No, granny. No human life goes to waste. If one of us dies before his time, his soul returns to the world to complete its span, to do the things left undone and experience the happiness and griefs he would have known. [*A pause.*] Granny, do you remember you told us how the dead go trooping at midnight into the synagogue? They go to pray the prayers they would have prayed in life, had they not died too soon. [*A pause.*] My mother died in her youth and had no time to live through all that lay in store for her. That is why I go today to the cemetery to ask her to join my father when he leads me under the wedding-canopy. She will be with me there, and after the ceremony we shall dance together. It is the same with all the souls who leave the world before their time. They are here in our midst, unheard and invisible. Only if your desire is strong enough, you can see them, and hear their voices and learn their thoughts. . . . I can. . . . [*Pointing to the grave.*] The holy grave—I have known it ever since I was a child. And I know the bride and bridegroom buried there. I've seen them often and often, sometimes in dreams and sometimes when I am wide awake. They are as near to me as my own people. . . . [*Deep in meditation.*] They were on the way to their wedding, so young and lovely to see, with a long and beautiful life before them.

But murderers set upon them with axes, and in a moment they both lay dead upon the ground. They were laid in one grave, so that they might be together for all time. [*She rises and goes to the grave, followed by* FRADE, GITTEL *and* BASSIA. *Stretching out her arms, she says in a loud voice.*] Holy bridegroom and bride, I invite you to my wedding. Be with me under the canopy.

[*Gay march music is heard in the distance.* LEAH *screams in terror and almost falls.* GITTEL *catches her.*]

GITTEL

What is it, Leah dear? Don't be frightened. They must be greeting the bridegroom with music as he comes into the village.

BASSIA

[*Excited.*]
I'm going to take a peep at him.

GITTEL

I, too. We'll run back, Leah, and tell you what he looks like. Shall we?

LEAH

[*Shaking her head.*]
No.

BASSIA

She's only shy. Little stupid, there's nothing to be ashamed of. . . . We won't give you away!

[*Exit* BASSIA *running, followed by* GITTEL.]

FRADE

[*Returning with* LEAH *to the stoop.*]

That is the custom, my child. The bride always sends her friend to see whether the groom is fair or dark, and . . .

MESSENGER

[*Approaching.*]

Bride!

LEAH

[*Shivers as she turns toward him.*]

Yes—what is it?

[*She gazes fixedly at him.*]

MESSENGER

The souls of the dead *do* return to earth, but not as disembodied spirits. Some must pass through many forms before they achieve purification. [LEAH *listens with ever-increasing attention.*] The souls of the wicked return in the forms of beasts, or birds, or fish—of plants even, and are powerless to purify themselves by their own efforts. They have to wait for the coming of some righteous sage to purge them of their sins and set them free. Others enter the bodies of the newly born, and cleanse themselves by well-doing.

LEAH

[*In tremulous eagerness.*]
Yes . . . yes. . . .

MESSENGER

Besides these, there are vagrant souls which, finding neither rest nor harbor, pass into the bodies of the living, in the form of a Dybbuk, until they have attained purity.
[*Exit the* MESSENGER.]

[LEAH *remains lost in astonishment, as* SENDER *comes out of the house.*]

SENDER

Why are you sitting here like this, little daughter?

FRADE

She entertained the beggars at their meal and danced with them afterwards. They tired her, so she is resting awhile now.

SENDER

Entertaining the poor, eh? That is a sweet and pious deed. [*He looks up at the sky.*] It is getting

very late but the bridegroom and his people have
arrived at last. Is everything ready?

FRADE

She has still to go to the grave-yard.

SENDER

Yes, go, my little one—go to Mamma. [*He sighs.*]
Let your tears fall on her grave and ask her to come
to your wedding. Ask her to be with you, so that we
may lead our only daughter under the canopy together. Say that I have fulfilled her dying wishes
to devote my life to you and bring you up to be a
true and virtuous daughter of Israel. This I have
done, and am now about to give you in marriage to a
learned and God-fearing young man, of good family.
  [*He wipes away his tears and with bowed head
  turns back into the house.*]

  [*A pause.*]

LEAH

Granny, may I invite others at the grave-yard besides mother?

FRADE

Only the near relations. You must ask your
grandfather, Rabbi Ephraim, and your Aunt Mirele.

LEAH

There is someone else I want to ask—not a
relation.

FRADE

No, daughter—that is forbidden. If you invite one stranger, the others might take offense and do you harm.

LEAH

He is not a stranger, granny. He was in our house like one of ourselves.

FRADE

[*In a voice low with fear.*]
Child, child—you fill me with fear. . . . They say he died a bad, unnatural death. [LEAH *weeps silently.*] There, there, my little one, don't cry. You shall ask him if you must; granny will take the sin upon herself. [*Bethinking herself.*] I don't know where they buried him, though, and it would never do to ask.

LEAH

I know where he is.

FRADE

[*Surprised.*]
You know? How?

LEAH

I saw his grave in a dream. [*She closes her eyes in a trance.*] And I saw him, too. He told me his trouble and begged me to invite him to the wedding.
[GITTEL *and* BASSIA *enter running.*]

GITTEL AND BASSIA

[*Together, in high excitement.*]

We've seen him—we've seen him!

LEAH

[*In consternation.*]

Whom—whom have you seen?

GITTEL

Why, the bridegroom, of course. And he's dark. . . .

BASSIA

No, he isn't—he's fair. . . .

GITTEL

Come, let's take another look and make sure. . . .

[*They run off.*]

LEAH

[*Rising.*]

Come, Granny—let us go to the graveyard.

FRADE

[*Sadly.*]

Yes, my baby. . . . Och, och, och!

[LEAH *takes a black shawl and puts it round her shoulders. With* FRADE *at her side, she passes slowly down the alley to the right. The stage remains empty for a moment. Music is heard approaching, as from the alley*

on the left come NACHMON, RABBI MENDEL
and MENASHE, *a small, wizened youth who
stares about him with wide, terrified eyes.
They are followed by relatives, men and
women, in holiday clothes.* SENDER *comes
out to meet them.*]

SENDER

[*Shakes* NACHMON's *hand warmly.*]
Sholom aleichem, Nachmon.   You are welcome.
[*They kiss.* SENDER *shakes hands with* MENASHE
*and kisses him.   He then shakes hands with the rest
of the party.*]   Have you had a good journey?

NACHMON

We have had a hard and bitter journey.   First we
missed the road and went astray in the fields.   Then
we plunged into a swamp which nearly swallowed us
up.   It was all we could do to pull ourselves out,
and the thought flashed through my mind that the
Evil Ones, God forbid, were at work to prevent our
getting here at all.   However, by the goodness of
God we have still managed to arrive in time.

SENDER

You must be exhausted.   Come in and rest.

NACHMON

There's no time to rest, we have still to settle the

details of the marriage-contract, the transfer of the dowry—the wedding gifts—how long the couple should live in the bridegroom's father's house, and so forth. . . .

SENDER

As you wish—I am entirely at your disposal.

[*Puts his arm around* NACHMON'S *shoulders, and walks up and down the square with him, talking.*]

RABBI MENDEL

[*To* MENASHE.]

Remember now—you are to remain perfectly quiet at the table. Keep your eyes downcast, and make no movement of any sort. The moment the supper is over, the master of ceremonies will call out: "The bridegroom will now deliver his oration." Then you will rise immediately and stand on the bench. Begin intoning loudly—the louder the better. And you are not to be bashful—do you hear?

MENASHE

Yes, I hear. [*In a frightened whisper.*] Rabbi, I'm afraid.

RABBI MENDEL

[*Alarmed.*]

Afraid—what of? Have you forgotten your oration?

MENASHE

No—it isn't that.

RABBI MENDEL

What then?

MENASHE

[*In anguish.*]

I don't know myself. But no sooner had we left home than I was seized with terror. All the places we passed were strange to me—I've never in my life seen so many unfamiliar faces. I can't stand the way they look at me—I'm afraid of their eyes. [*He shudders.*] Rabbi, nothing terrifies me so much as the eyes of strangers.

RABBI MENDEL

I'll pray that the evil eye be averted from you.

MENASHE

Rabbi, I'd like to stay alone, I'd like to creep into a corner somewhere. But here I'm surrounded by strangers. I have to talk to them, answer their questions; I feel as if I were being dragged to the gallows. [*With mystic terror.*] Rabbi, above all, I'm frightened of her, the maiden.

RABBI MENDEL

Make up your mind to master your fears, and you will. Otherwise, God forbid, you may forget your oration. Let us go to the inn now, and I will hear you go over it again.

MENASHE

[*Clutches at Mendel's hand.*]

Rabbi—what's that grave there in the middle of the street?

> [*They read the inscription on the headstone in silence, and stand for a moment beside the grave; then with bowed heads pass down the alley to the left.* SENDER, NACHMON *and the* WEDDING GUEST *enter the house. The poor file out of the courtyard, with their bags on their shoulders and staves in their hands. They cross the square silently and vanish down the alley to the left. A few linger in the square.*]

A TALL PALE WOMAN

Now the poor people's feast is over—like all the other things—just as if they'd never been.

LAME OLD WOMAN

They said there'd be a plate of soup for everyone, but there wasn't.

A HUNCHBACK

And only little slices of white bread.

A MAN ON CRUTCHES

A rich man like him—as if it would have hurt him to give us a whole loaf each.

THE TALL WOMAN

They might have given us a bit of chicken. Just look, chicken *and* geese *and* turkeys for their rich guests.

A HALF-BLIND WOMAN

Oh, what does it matter? It all goes to the worms when we're dead. Och, och, och!

[*They go slowly out. The stage is empty for a moment. Then the* MESSENGER *crosses from the left and enters the synagogue. Dusk is falling. The shopkeepers are closing for the night. In the synagogue and at* SENDER's *house, lights are appearing.* SENDER, GITTEL *and* BASSIA *come onto the stoop. They peer about.*]

SENDER

[*Worried.*]

Where is Leah? Where is old Frade? How is it they aren't back from the graveyard all this time? Can they have met with an accident, God forbid?

GITTEL AND BASSIA

We'll go and meet them.

[*From the alley on the right,* FRADE *and* LEAH *come hurrying.*]

FRADE

Hurry, child, hurry! Ei, ei—how long we've been! Oh, why did I let you have your way? I am so afraid something dreadful is going to happen, God forbid!

SENDER

Oh, here they are. What can have kept you all this time?

[*Women come out of the house.*]

WOMEN

Bring in the bride to pray before the candles.

[LEAH *is led into the house.*]

FRADE

[*Whispering to* GITTEL *and* BASSIA.]

She fainted. I'd a hard time bringing her round. I'm shaking all over still.

BASSIA

That's because she's been fasting . . . it weakens the heart.

GITTEL

Did she cry much at her mother's grave?

FRADE

Better not ask what happened there. I'm still shaking all over. . . .

[*A chair is set near the door and* LEAH *is led out. They seat her. Music.* NACHMON, MENASHE, RABBI MENDEL *and the guests approach from the alley on the left.* ME-*

NASHE *carries a cloth over his outstretched hands, and crosses to* LEAH *in order to cover her face with it. The* MESSENGER *comes out of the synagogue.*]

LEAH

[*Tears the cloth away, and springing up, thrusts* MENASHE *from her, crying out.*]
No! YOU are not my bridegroom!
[*General consternation. They all crowd round* LEAH.]

SENDER

[*Overwhelmed.*]
Little daughter, what is it, my darling? What has come over you?
[LEAH *breaks away from them and runs to the grave, reaching out her arms.*]

LEAH

Holy bridegroom and bride, protect me—save me! [*She falls. They flock round her, and raise her from the ground. She looks wildly about, and cries out, not in her natural voice, but in the voice of a man.*] Ah! Ah! You buried me. But I have come back—to my destined bride. I will leave her no more! [NACHMON *crosses to* LEAH, *and she shrieks into his face.*] Chamilouk!

NACHMON

[*Trembling.*]
She has gone mad.

MESSENGER

Into the bride has entered a Dybbuk.
[*Great tumult.*]

CURTAIN

ACT III

Miropol. A large room in the house of RABBI
AZRAEL *of Miropol. Right, door leading to
other rooms. In middle of wall, center, door to
street. On either side of this door, benches.
Windows. Left, a table almost the entire
length of the wall, covered with a white cloth.
On table, slices of white bread.* At the head of
table, a great armchair. Past the door right, a
small cupboard containing scrolls of the law.
Beside it, an altar. Opposite, a small table,
sofa, and several chairs.*

*It is the Sabbath—evening prayers are just
over.* CHASSIDIM *go to and fro in the room while*
ELDER MICHOEL *places about the table the
pieces of white bread. The* MESSENGER *is sitting beside the cupboard where the scrolls are,
surrounded by a group of* CHASSIDIM. *Others
sit apart, reading. Two stand beside the
small table. A low chanting is heard from an*

---

* Sabbath bread which is prayed over at the close of the
Sabbath.

94

inner room: "*God of Abraham, Isaac and Jacob . . .*" *The two* CHASSIDIM *speak.*

FIRST CHASSID

He has some wonderful tales, the Stranger. It gives you the creeps to listen to them—I'm afraid to, myself.

SECOND CHASSID

What are they about?

FIRST CHASSID

They're full of deep meaning, but it's not easy to grasp what the meaning is. For all *we* know, they may have something to do with the Bratslaver's creed.*

SECOND CHASSID

There can't be anything very heretical in them if the older Chassidim can listen to him.

[*They join the group about the* MESSENGER.]

THIRD CHASSID

Go on---tell us another . . .

MESSENGER

It is late. There is hardly any time left.

* Nachmon Bratslaver, a descendant of Balshem, the founder of Chassidism. Bratslaver was a famous Rabbi, a poet and philosopher.

FOURTH CHASSID

That's all right. The Rabbi won't be here for a good while yet.

MESSENGER

[*Continuing his stories.*]

Well, then. At the end of the earth stands a high mountain; on the top of this mountain is a huge boulder, and out of the boulder flows a stream of clear water. At the opposite end of the earth is the heart of the world. Now each thing in the world has a heart, and the world itself has a great heart of its own. And the heart of the world keeps the clear stream ever in sight, gazing at it with insatiable longing and desire. But the heart of the world can make not even one step toward it, for the moment it stirs from its place, it loses sight of the mountain's summit and the crystal spring. And if, though for a single instant only, it lose sight of the spring, it loses in that same moment its life, and the heart of the world begins to die.

The crystal spring has no life-span of its own, but endures only so long as the heart of the world allows. And this is one day only.

Now at the close of day, the spring calls to the heart of the world in a song and is answered in a song from the heart. And the sound of their song passes over all the earth, and out of it shining threads come forth and fasten onto the hearts of all the world's creatures and from one heart to another.

There is a righteous and benevolent man who goes to and fro over all the earth's surface, gathering up the threads from all the hearts. These he weaves into Time, and when he has woven one whole day, he passes it over to the heart of the world, which passes it over to the crystal spring, and so the spring achieves another day of life.

THIRD CHASSID

The Rabbi is coming.

[*Silence falls. They all rise.* RABBI AZRAEL *enters at door, left. He is a man of great age, dressed in a white kaftan and high fur cap. Very slowly and wearily, deep in thought, he crosses to the table, and sinks into the arm-chair at its head.* MICHOEL *takes his place at the rabbi's right hand, and the* CHASSIDIM *group themselves around the table, the elders sitting, the younger standing behind them.* MICHOEL *distributes white bread.* RABBI AZRAEL *lifts his head, and in a low, quavering voice chants.*]

RABBI AZRAEL

The feast of David, the King, the Messiah . . . [*The others make the response and say grace over the bread. They begin chanting in low tones, a sad, mysterious air without words. There is a pause.* RABBI AZRAEL *sighs deeply, rests his head on both* *hands, and in that position remains seated, lost in meditation. An atmosphere of suspense pervades the silence. At last,* RABBI AZRAEL *again raises his head, and begins to intone.*] It is told of the holy Balshem *—may his merits hover over us . . . [*There is a momentary pause.*] One day there came to Meshibach a troupe of German acrobats who gave their performance in the streets of the town. They stretched a rope across the river and one of them walked along the rope to the opposite bank. From all sides the people came running to behold this ungodly marvel, and in the midst of the crowd of onlookers stood the holy Balshem himself. His disciples were greatly astonished, and asked him the meaning of his presence there. And the holy Balshem answered them thus: I went to see how a man might cross the chasm between two heights as this man did, and as I watched him I reflected that if mankind would submit their souls to such discipline as that to which he submitted his body, what deep abysses might they not cross upon the tenuous cord of life!

> [*The* RABBI *sighs deeply. In the pause that follows, the* CHASSIDIM *exchange enraptured glances.*]

FIRST CHASSID

Lofty as the world!

* The founder of the Chassidic Sect.

SECOND CHASSID

Wonder of Wonders!

THIRD CHASSID

Glory of glories!

RABBI AZRAEL

[*To* MICHOEL, *whispering.*]
There is a stranger here.

MICHOEL

[*Looking round.*]
He is a messenger, in the confidence of the Great
Ones.

RABBI AZRAEL

What message does he bring?

MICHOEL

I don't know. Shall I tell him to go away?

RABBI AZRAEL

God forbid! A stranger must, on the contrary,
be shown special honor. Give him a chair.
[*Pause.*] The world of God is great and holy. In
all the world the holiest land is the Land of Israel.
In the Land of Israel the holiest city is Jerusalem;
in Jerusalem the holiest place was the holy Temple,
and the holiest spot in the Temple was the Holy of
Holies. [*He pauses.*] In the world there are seventy
nations, and of them the holiest is Israel. The holiest

of the people of Israel is the tribe of the Levites.
The holiest of the Levites are the priests, and
amongst the priests, the holiest is the High Priest.
[*Pause.*]   The year has three hundred and fifty-four
days.   Of these the holidays are the holiest.   Holier
than the holidays are the Sabbaths and the holiest of
the Sabbaths is Yom Kippur,* Sabbath of Sabbaths.
[*Pause.*]   There are in the world seventy tongues.
The holiest of these is the holy tongue of Israel.   The
holiest of all things written in this tongue is the Holy
Torah; of the Torah the holiest part is the Ten Commandments, and the holiest of all the words in the Ten
Commandments is the Name of the Lord.   [*Pause.*]
At a certain hour, on a certain day of the year, all
these four supreme holinesses met together.   This
took place on the Day of Atonement, at the hour
when the High Priest entered the Holy of Holies and
there revealed the Divine Name.   And as this hour
was holy and terrible beyond words, so also was it the
hour of utmost peril for the High Priest, and for the
entire commonweal of Israel.   For if, in that hour
(which God forbid), a sinful or a wayward thought
had entered the mind of the High Priest, it would
have brought the destruction of the world.   [*Pause.*]
Wherever a man stand to lift his eyes to heaven, that
place is a Holy of Holies.   Every human being created by God in His own image and likeness is a High
Priest.   Each day of a man's life is the Day of Atone-
* The Day of Atonement.

ment; and every word he speaks from his heart is the name of the Lord. Therefore the sin of any man, whether of commission or of omission, brings the ruin of a whole world in its train. [*His voice becomes weaker and trembles.*] Through many transmigrations, the human soul is drawn by pain and grief, as the child to its mother's breast, to the source of its being, the Exalted Throne above. But it happens sometimes that a soul which has attained to the final state of purification suddenly becomes the prey of evil forces which cause it to slip and fall. And the higher it had soared, the deeper it falls. And with the fall of such a soul as this, a world plunges to ruin. And darkness overwhelms the spheres. The ten spheres bewail the world that is lost. [*He pauses, and seems to awaken to consciousness.*] My children, tonight we will shorten the seeing out of the Queen.*

> [*All except* MICHOEL *silently leave the room, the spell of the Rabbi's discourses still upon them.*]

MICHOEL
[*Approaches the table uncertainly.*]
Rabbi . . . Rabbi, Sender of Brainitz is here.

RABBI AZRAEL
[*Mechanically repeating the words.*]
Sender of Brainitz . . . I know.

---

* The Sabbath is the Queen, whose going is celebrated with prayer.

MICHOEL

A terrible misfortune has befallen him. A Dybbuk —God's mercy be upon us—has entered into his daughter.

RABBI AZRAEL

A Dybbuk has . . . I know.

MICHOEL

He has brought her to you.

RABBI AZRAEL

[*As if to himself.*]

To me? . . . To me? . . . Why to me, when there *is* no me to come to? For I am myself no longer.

MICHOEL

But Rabbi—everybody comes to you—a world of people.

RABBI AZRAEL

As you say—a world of people. Yes, a blind world—blind sheep following a blind shepherd. If they had eyes to see with, they would seek guidance not from me, but from Him who alone can justly use the word "I," for He is, in all the world, the only "I."

MICHOEL

You are His representative, Rabbi.

RABBI AZRAEL

So says the world. But as for me, I do not
know. For forty years I have sat in the Rabbi's
chair, and yet, to this very day I am not convinced
that I am indeed the appointed deputy on earth of
Him whose Name be praised. At times I am con-
scious of my nearness to the All. Then I am free of
doubts, and feel the power within me—then I know
I am master over the high worlds. But there are
other times when that certainty abandons me, and
then I am as small and feeble as a child, then I myself, and not those who come to me, need help.

MICHOEL

I know, Rabbi—I remember. Once you came to
me at midnight, and asked me to recite the psalms
with you. All the night long, we said them together,
weeping.

RABBI AZRAEL

That was a long time ago—it is worse than ever
now. [*His voice fails.*] What do they want of me?
I am old and weak. My body has earned its rest—
my soul longs for solitude. Yet still they come
thronging to me, all the misery and sorrow of the
world. Each imploring word pierces my flesh like a
thorn . . . No, I have no longer the strength . . .
I cannot . . .

MICHOEL

[*Filled with fear.*]
Rabbi, Rabbi! . . .

RABBI AZRAEL

[*Suddenly breaking into tears.*]
I can't go on . . . I can't . . .
[*He weeps.*]

MICHOEL

Rabbi—do you forget the generations of righteous
and holy men of God from whom you are descended?
Your father, Rabbi Itzele, blessed be his name, your
grandfather, our master and lord—our teacher,
Rabbi Velvele the Great, who was a pupil of the Holy
Balshem himself . . .

RABBI AZRAEL

[*Regaining his self-control.*]
No—I will not forget my forebears—my holy
father who three times had a revelation direct from
God; my uncle, Rabbi Meyer Baer, who upon the
words of "Hear, O Israel" could ascend to Heaven at
will; the great Velvele, my grandfather, who resur-
rected the dead . . . [*All his spirit has returned as
he speaks to* MICHOEL.] Michoel, do you know that
my grandfather would drive out Dybbuks without
either spells or incantations—with a single word of
command, only one, he expelled them. In times of

stress I always turn to him, and he sustains me.   He will not forsake me now.   Call in Sender.

[MICHOEL *goes, and returns in a moment with* SENDER.]

SENDER

[*Tearfully, with outspread hands.*]

Rabbi!   Have mercy on me!   Help me!   Save my only daughter!

RABBI AZRAEL

How did this misfortune come upon you?

SENDER

Just as they were about to veil the bride, and . . .

RABBI AZRAEL

That is not what I asked.   Tell me, what could have brought this thing to pass?   A worm can enter a fruit only after it has begun to rot.

SENDER

Rabbi, my only daughter is a pious Jewish maiden. She is modest and gentle—she has never disobeyed me.

RABBI AZRAEL

Children are sometimes punished for the sins of their parents.

SENDER

If I knew of any sin I had committed, I would do penance for it.

RABBI AZRAEL

Have you asked the Dybbuk who he was, and why he entered into your daughter?

SENDER

He refuses to answer. But we recognized him by his voice. He was a student in our *yeshiva* who died suddenly in the synagogue. That was months ago. He had been meddling in the Kabala and came to grief through it.

RABBI AZRAEL

What powers destroyed him?

SENDER

Evil ones, they say. An hour or two before his death, he had been telling a fellow-student that sin need not be fought against, for Satan too is holy at the core. He also tried the use of charms to obtain two barrels of gold.

RABBI AZRAEL

Did you know him?

SENDER

Yes. I was one of those in whose house he stayed.

RABBI AZRAEL

[*Bending his gaze intently upon* SENDER.]

You may have put some slight upon him or mistreated him. Try to remember.

SENDER

I don't know . . . I can't remember . . . [*Desperately.*] Rabbi, I'm only human, after all . . . I . . .

RABBI AZRAEL

Bring in the maiden.

> [SENDER *goes out and returns immediately with* FRADE, *who supports* LEAH. LEAH *stops in the doorway and will go no further.*]

SENDER

> [*Weeping.*]

Have pity on your father, my child—don't put him to shame before the Rabbi. Come inside.

FRADE

Go in, Leah dear—go in, little dove.

LEAH

I want to . . . but I can't . . .

RABBI AZRAEL

Maiden, I command you—come in! [LEAH *advances into the room and crosses to the table.*] Sit down!

LEAH

> [*Does as the* RABBI *tells her. Then suddenly springs up and cries out with a voice not her own.*]

Let me be! I will not be here!

[*She tries to escape, but is stopped by* SENDER *and* FRADE.]

RABBI AZRAEL

Dybbuk! Who are you? I command you to answer.

LEAH

[*In the voice of the* DYBBUK.]

Miropol Rabbi—you know very well who I am. I do not wish the others to know.

RABBI AZRAEL

I do not ask your name—I ask: Who *are* you?

LEAH

[*As before.*]

I am one of those who sought other paths.

RABBI AZRAEL

He only seeks other paths who has lost the straight one.

LEAH

[*As before.*]

The straight one is too narrow.

RABBI AZRAEL

That has been said before by one who did not return. [*Pause.*] Why did you enter into this maiden?

LEAH

[*As before.*]
I am her predestined bridegroom.

RABBI AZRAEL

According to our Holy Scriptures, a dead soul
may not stay in the realms of the living.

LEAH

[*As before.*]
I have not died.

RABBI AZRAEL

You left our world, and so are forbidden to return
until the blast of the great trumpet shall be heard.
I command you therefore to leave the body of this
maiden, in order that a living branch of the im-
perishable tree of Israel may not be blasted.

LEAH

[*Shrieks in the* DYBBUK's *voice.*]
Miropol Rabbi—I know your almighty power. I
know that angels and archangels obey your word.
But me you cannot command. I have nowhere to go.
Every road is barred against me and every gate is
locked. On every side, the forces of evil lie in wait
to seize me. [*In a trembling voice.*] There is
heaven, and there is earth—and all the countless
worlds in space, yet in not one of these is there any

place for me.   And now that my soul has found
refuge from the bitterness and terror of pursuit, you
wish to drive me away.   Have mercy!   Do not send
me away—don't force me to go!

RABBI AZRAEL

I am filled with profound pity for you, wandering
soul!   And I will use all my power to save you from
the evil spirits.   But the body of this maiden you
must leave.

LEAH

[*In the* DYBBUK's *voice, firmly.*)
I refuse!

RABBI AZRAEL

Michoel.   Summon a *minyen* from the synagogue.
[MICHOEL *returns at once with ten Jews who take
their places on one side of the room.*]   Holy Community, do you give me authority to cast out of
the body of a Jewish maiden, in your behalf and with
your power, a spirit which refuses to leave her of its
own free will?

THE TEN

Rabbi, we give you authority to cast out of the
body of a Jewish maiden, in our behalf and in our
name and with our power, a spirit which refuses to
leave her of its own free will.

RABBI

[Rises.]

Dybbuk! Soul of one who has left the world in which we live! In the name and with the power of a holy community of Jews, I, Azrael, son of Itzele, order you to depart out of the body of the maiden, Leah, daughter of Channah, and in departing, to do no injury either to her or to any other living being. If you do not obey me, I shall proceed against you with malediction and anathema, to the limit of my powers, and with the utmost might of my uplifted arm. But if you do as I command you, then I shall bend all my strength to drive away the fiends and evil spirits that surround you, and keep you safe from them.

LEAH

[Shrieks in the voice of the DYBBUK.]

I'm not afraid of your anathema. I put no faith in your promises. The power is not in the world that can help me. The loftiest height of the world cannot compare with this resting-place that I have found, nor is there in the world an abysm so fathomless as that which waits to receive me if ever I leave my only refuge. I will not go.

RABBI AZRAEL

In the name of the Almighty, I adjure you for the last time. Leave the body of this maiden— If you do not, I shall utter the anathema against you and deliver you into the hands of the fiends of destruction.

[*An ominous pause.*]

LEAH

[*In the voice of the* DYBBUK.]
In the name of the Almighty, I am bound to my betrothed, and will remain with her to all eternity.

RABBI AZRAEL

Michoel, have white shrouds brought for all who are here. Bring seven trumpets . . . and seven black candles . . . Then seven holy scrolls from their place.
[*A pause fraught with dire omen, during which* MICHOEL *goes out and returns with trumpets and black candles. The* MESSENGER *follows him with the shrouds.*]

MESSENGER

[*Counting the shrouds.*]
One too many. [*He looks round the room.*] Someone is missing, perhaps?

RABBI AZRAEL

[*Worried—as if recalling something.*]
Before pronouncing the anathema against a Jewish soul, it is necessary to obtain the permission of the City Rabbi. Michoel, leave these things for the

present. Here is my staff. Take it and go to the City Rabbi, and ask him to come without delay.

[MICHOEL *puts the trumpets and candles aside and goes out with the* MESSENGER, *who still carries the shrouds over his arm.*]

RABBI AZRAEL

[*To the ten.*]
Wait outside until they come back. [*They leave the room. There is a pause.* RABBI AZRAEL *turns to* SENDER.] Sender, where are the bridegroom and his people?

SENDER

They stayed in Brainitz over the Sabbath, at my house.

RABBI AZRAEL

Let a messenger ride over and tell them in my name, to stay there and await my orders.

SENDER

I'll send at once.

RABBI AZRAEL

You may leave me now, and take the maiden into the next room.

LEAH

[*Wakes out of her trance, and speaks in her own voice, trembling.*]
Granny—I'm frightened. What are they going to do to him? What are they going to do to me?

FRADE

There, there, my child—you've nothing to be frightened of. The Rabbi knows best. He couldn't harm anyone. The Rabbi can't do wrong, my darling.

[FRADE *and* SENDER *take* LEAH *into the adjoining room.*]

RABBI AZRAEL

[*Remains absorbed in his thoughts. Then he looks up.*]

Even though it has been thus ordained in the high planes, I will reverse that destiny.

[*Enter* RABBI SAMSON.]

RABBI SAMSON

A good week to you, Rabbi.

RABBI AZRAEL

[*Rises to meet him.*]

A good week, a good year to you, Rabbi. Be seated. [RABBI SAMSON *takes a seat.*] I have troubled you to come here in a very grave matter. A Dybbuk (the Lord of Mercy be with us), has entered into a daughter of Israel, and nothing will induce him to leave her. Only the last resort is left, to force him out by anathema, and this I ask your permission to do. The salvation of a soul will thereby be added to your other merits.

RABBI SAMSON

[*Sighing.*]

Anathema is cruel punishment enough for the living—it is far more so for the dead. But if, as you say, all other means have failed, and so godly a man as yourself believe it necessary, I give you my consent. I have a secret, however, which I must reveal to you, Rabbi, for it has a vital bearing on this affair.

RABBI AZRAEL

I am listening, Rabbi.

RABBI SAMSON

Rabbi, do you remember a young Chassid from Brainitz, Nissin ben Rifke by name, who used to come to you from time to time, about twenty years ago?

RABBI AZRAEL

Yes. He went away to some place a long way off and died there, still in his youth.

RABBI SAMSON

That is he. Well, that same Nissin ben Rifke appeared to me three times in my dreams last night, demanding that I summon Sender of Brainitz to trial before the Rabbinical Court.

RABBI AZRAEL

What was his charge against Sender?

RABBI SAMSON

He did not state it to me.　He only kept saying that Sender had done him a mortal injury.

RABBI AZRAEL

A rabbi can obviously not prevent any Jew from summoning another to appear before the court, particularly when the complainant is dead and could appeal in the last resort to the Highest Tribunal of all . . . But how do these visitations of yours affect this Dybbuk?

RABBI SAMSON

In this manner . . . It has come to my ears that the youth who died and entered into the body of Sender's daughter as a Dybbuk, was Nissin ben Rifke's only son . . . There is also some rumor concerning a pact with Nissin ben Rifke which has not been kept.

RABBI AZRAEL

[*After a moment's reflection.*]

This being the case, I shall postpone the exorcising of the Dybbuk until tomorrow midday.　In the morning after prayers, you shall summon the dead man to court, and God willing, we shall discover the reason for his visitations to you.　And then, with your permission, I shall cast out the Dybbuk by anathema.

RABBI SAMSON

In view of the difficulty of a trial between a living

man and a dead one, which is as rare as it is difficult, I beg that you will preside over the court, Rabbi, and conduct the proceedings.

RABBI AZRAEL

Very well . . . Michoel. [*Enter* MICHOEL.] Bring in the maiden. [SENDER *and* FRADE *bring* LEAH *into the room. She sits down before the* RABBI *with her eyes closed.*] Dybbuk! I give you respite until noon tomorrow. If at that hour you persist in your refusal to leave this maiden's body of your own accord, I shall, with the permission of the City Rabbi, tear you away from her with the utmost force of the *cherem.** [SENDER *and* FRADE *lead* LEAH *towards the door.*] Sender, you are to remain.

[FRADE *takes* LEAH *out.*]

Sender, do you remember the bosom friend of your youth—Nissin ben Rifke?

SENDER

[*Frightened.*]
Nissin ben Rifke? He died, didn't he?

RABBI AZRAEL

Know then that he appeared three times last night before the Rabbi of the City [*indicating* RABBI SAMSON] as he slept. And Nissin ben Rifke de-

* The sentence of excommunication.

manded that you be summoned to stand trial by the Rabbinical Court for a wrong that you have done him.

SENDER

[*Stunned.*]

Me? A trial? Is there no end to my misfortunes? What does he want of me? Rabbi, help me! What shall I do?

RABBI AZRAEL

I do not know the nature of his charge. But you must accept the summons.

SENDER

I will do whatever you say.

RABBI AZRAEL

[*In a different tone.*]

Let the swiftest horses be sent immediately to Brainitz, to fetch the bridegroom and his people. Have them here before midday tomorrow, in order that the wedding may take place as soon as the Dybbuk has been expelled. Have the canopy set up.

SENDER

Rabbi! What if they no longer wish to be connected with my family, and refuse to come?

[*The* MESSENGER *appears in the doorway.*]

RABBI AZRAEL

[*With dignity.*]

Tell them *I* have commanded them to come. Let nothing prevent the bridegroom from arriving in time.

MESSENGER

The bridegroom will be here in time.

[*The clock strikes twelve.*]

CURTAIN

ACT IV

SAME SCENE AS ACT III

Instead of the long table, left, a smaller one nearer to footlights. RABBI AZRAEL, *wrapped in his prayer shawl and wearing the phylacteries, is in the armchair. The two* JUDGES *sit in ordinary chairs.* RABBI SAMSON *stands beside the table and, at a distance,* MICHOEL. *They are finishing a prayer whereby an evil dream may be turned into good.*

RABBI AZRAEL, MICHOEL AND THE TWO JUDGES

You beheld a good dream! You beheld a good dream! You beheld a good dream!

RABBI AZRAEL

We have found a solution of good to your dream.

RABBI SAMSON

I beheld a good dream—a good dream I beheld. I beheld a good dream.

120

RABBI AZRAEL

Will you now, Rabbi Samson, take your seat with the other judges? [RABBI SAMSON *sits down next to* RABBI AZRAEL.] Let us now call upon this dead man to be present at the trial. First, however, I shall draw a holy circle beyond which he may not pass. Michoel, my staff. . . . [MICHOEL *gives him the staff.* RABBI AZRAEL *then rises and, going to the corner left, describes a circle on the floor from left to right. He then returns to the table.*] Michoel, take my staff and go to the graveyard. When you get there, go in with your eyes closed, guiding yourself with the staff. At the first grave it touches, stop. Knock with it three times upon this grave, and repeat what I shall tell you faithfully word for word: Pure dead, I am sent by Azrael, son of the great sage, Rabbi Itzele of Miropol, to beg you to pardon him for disturbing your peace, and to deliver his command that you inform the pure dead, Nissin ben Rifke, by means known to you as follows: That the just and righteous Rabbinical Court of Miropol summons him to be present immediately at a trial at which he shall appear in the same garb as that in which he was buried. Repeat these words three times; then turn and come back here. You will not look behind you, no matter what cries or calls or shrieks may pursue you, nor will you allow my staff to leave your hand even for one moment, otherwise you will place yourself in dire peril. Go and God will protect you, for no harm can come to him who is bound on a virtuous errand. But before you go, let two men come in and make a partition which shall separate the dead man from the living. [MICHOEL *goes out. Two* MEN *enter with a sheet with which they screen the left-hand corner down to the floor. They then leave the room.*] Let Sender come in. [SENDER *appears.*] Sender, have you carried out my instructions and sent horses for the bridegroom and his people?

SENDER

The swiftest horses were sent, but the bridegroom has not yet arrived.

RABBI AZRAEL

Have someone ride out to meet them and say they are to drive as fast as they can.

SENDER

Yes, Rabbi.
[*Pause.*]

RABBI AZRAEL

Sender, we have sent to inform the pure dead, Nissin ben Rifke, that the Rabbinical Court summons him to appear in his cause against you. Are you willing to accept our verdict?

SENDER

I am.

RABBI AZRAEL

Will you carry out our sentence?

SENDER

I will.

RABBI AZRAEL

Then step back and take your place upon the right.

SENDER

Rabbi, it begins to come back to me. . . . It may be that the trial which Nissin ben Rifke has summoned me to, concerns an agreement upon which we shook hands one day many years ago. But in that matter I am not to blame.

RABBI AZRAEL

You will have an opportunity to speak of this later on, after the complainant has made known his grievance. [*Pause.*] Very soon there is personally to appear in our midst, a man from the True World, in order to submit to our judgment a case between himself and a man of our Untrue World. [*Pause.*] A trial such as this is proof that the laws set forth in the Holy Scriptures rule all worlds and all peoples, and unite both the living and the dead within their bonds. [*Pause.*] A trial such as this is difficult and terrible. The eyes of all the worlds are turned towards it, and should this court deviate from the Law by so much as a hair's breadth, tumult would ensue in the Court on High. It is with fear and trembling, therefore, that we are to approach the trial at issue . . . with fear and trembling. . . .

> [*He looks anxiously around him and as he does encounters the partition in the left-hand corner. He ceases to speak. There is a silence of awe.*]

FIRST JUDGE

> [*In a frightened whisper to the* SECOND JUDGE.]

I believe he's come.

SECOND JUDGE

> [*In the same tone.*]

It seems so.

RABBI SAMSON

He is here.

RABBI AZRAEL

Pure dead Nissin ben Rifke! You are commanded by this just and righteous court to stay within the circle and partition assigned to you, and not to go beyond them. Pure dead Nissin ben Rifke, you are commanded by this just and righteous court to state your grievance and the redress you seek against the accused, Sender ben Henie.

> [*Awestruck pause. All listen as though turned to stone.*]

FIRST JUDGE

I believe he is answering.

SECOND JUDGE

It seems so.

FIRST JUDGE

I hear a voice but no words.

SECOND JUDGE

And I words but no voice.

RABBI SAMSON

[*To* SENDER.]

Sender ben Henie, the pure dead Nissin ben Rifke
makes demand saying that in the years of your
youth you and he were students in the same *yeshiva*,
comrades, and that your soul and his were bound
together in true friendship. You were both married
in the same week, and when you met at the house of
the Rabbi, during the Great Holidays, you made a
solemn pact that if the wife of one of you should
conceive and bear a boy and the other a girl, those
two children should marry.

SENDER

[*In a tremulous voice.*]

It was so.

RABBI SAMSON

The pure dead Nissin ben Rifke makes further
demand, saying that soon afterwards he left for a
place very far away, where his wife bore him a son
in the same hour as your wife gave you a daughter.

Soon thereafter he was gathered to his fathers. [*Short pause.*] In the True World, he found that his son had been blest with a noble and lofty soul, and was progressing upwards from plane to plane, and at this his paternal heart overflowed with joy and pride. He also found that his son, growing older, had become a wanderer from province to province, and from country to country, and from city to city, for the soul to which his soul had been predestined was drawing him ever onward. At last he came to the city in which you dwell, and you took him into your house. He sat at your table, and his soul bound itself to the soul of your daughter. But you were rich, while Nissin's son was poor, and so you turned your back on him and went seeking for your daughter a bridegroom of high estate and great possessions. [*Short pause.*] Nissin then beheld his son grow desperate and become a wanderer once more, seeking now the New Paths. And sorrow and alarm filled his father's soul lest the dark powers, aware of the youth's extremity, spread their net for him. This they did, and caught him, and tore him from the world before his time. Thereafter the soul of Nissin ben Rifke's son roamed amidst the worlds until at last it entered as a Dybbuk into the body of his predestined. Nissin ben Rifke claims that the death of his son has severed him from both worlds, leaving him without name or memorial, since neither heir nor friend remains on earth to pray for his soul. His light has been extinguished forever—the crown of his head has rolled down into the abyss. Therefore, he begs the just and righteous court to pass sentence upon Sender according to the laws of our Holy Scriptures, for his shedding of the blood of Nissin's son and of his son's sons to the end of all generations.

[*An awestruck pause.* SENDER *is shaken with sobs.*]

RABBI AZRAEL

Sender ben Henie, have you heard the complaint brought against you by the holy dead, Nissin ben Rifke? What have you to say in answer to it?

SENDER

I can't speak . . . I have no words to say . . . in justification. But I would ask you to beg my old comrade to forgive me this sin, because it was not committed in malice. Soon after we had shaken hands upon our pact, Nissin went away, and I did not know whether his wife had had a child, either boy or girl. Then I received news of his death, but none about his family. And gradually the whole affair of our agreement went out of my mind.

RABBI AZRAEL

Why did you not inquire about him? Why did you make no inquiry?

SENDER

It is customary for the bridegroom's father to make the first advances, not the bride's. I thought that if Nissin had had a son, he would have let me know.

[*Pause.*]

RABBI SAMSON

Nissin ben Rifke asks why, when you received his son into your house and had him sit at your table, did you never ask him whence he came and of what family?

SENDER

I don't know. . . . I don't remember. . . . But I do swear that something urged me continually to take him for my son-in-law. That was why, whenever a match was proposed, I always made such hard conditions that the bridegroom's father would never agree to them. Three marriages fell through in this manner. But this time the bridegroom's people would not be put off.

[*Pause.*]

RABBI SAMSON

Nissin ben Rifke says that in your heart of hearts you were aware of his son's identity and therefore feared to ask him who he was. You were ambitious that your daughter should live in ease and riches, and for that reason thrust his son down into the abyss.

[SENDER *weeps silently, covering his face. There is a heavy pause.* MICHOEL *returns and gives the staff back to* RABBI AZRAEL.]

RABBI AZRAEL

[*After a whispered conference with* RABBI SAMSON *and the* JUDGES, *rises and takes the staff in his hand.*]

This just and righteous court has heard both parties and delivers its verdict as follows: Whereas it is not known whether, at the time Nissin ben Rifke and Sender ben Henie shook hands upon their agreement, their wives had already conceived; and whereas, according to our Holy Scriptures, no agreement whatsoever which involves anything not yet in existence can be held valid in law, we may not therefore find that this agreement was binding upon Sender. Since, however, in the Upper World, the agreement was accepted as valid and never canceled; and since the belief was implanted in the heart of Nissin ben Rifke's son that the daughter of Sender ben Henie was his predestined bride; and whereas, Sender ben Henie's subsequent conduct brought calamity upon Nissin ben Rifke and his son; Now, therefore, be it decreed by this just and righteous court, that Sender give the half of his fortune in alms to the poor, and each year, for the remainder

of his life, light the memorial candle for Nissin ben
Rifke and his son as though they were his own kin-
dred, and pray for their souls. [*Pause.*] The just
and righteous court now requests the holy dead,
Nissin ben Rifke, to forgive Sender unreservedly,
and to command his son in filial duty to leave the
body of the maiden, Leah, daughter of Channah, in
order that a branch of the fruitful tree of Israel may
not be blighted. In return for these things, the
Almighty will make manifest his grace to Nissin ben
Rifke and to his lost son.

ALL

Amen!

RABBI AZRAEL

Pure dead Nissin ben Rifke, have you heard our
judgment? Do you accept it? [*Pause.*] Sender
ben Henie, have you heard our judgment? Do you
accept it?

SENDER

I accept.

RABBI AZRAEL

Pure dead, Nissin ben Rifke, the trial between you
and Sender ben Henie is now ended. Do you return
therefore to your resting place, and in going we
command you to do no harm to man nor other living
creature whatsoever. [*Pause.*] Michoel, water.
. . . And have the curtain taken away. [MICHOEL
calls in TWO MEN, *who remove the sheet.* RABBI

AZRAEL *traces a circle in the same place as before, but from right to left. The* MEN *return with basin and ewer, and all wash their hands.*] Sender, have the bridegroom and his people arrived?

SENDER

There has been no sign of them.

RABBI AZRAEL

Send another rider to meet them, and say they are to press on with all the speed their horses can make. Have the canopy raised and the musicians in readiness. Let the bride be dressed in her wedding-gown so that the moment the Dybbuk has been cast out you may lead her under the canopy. What is now about to be done—will be done.

[*Sender goes out.* RABBI AZRAEL *takes off his prayer-shawl and phylacteries, folding them up.*]

RABBI SAMSON

[*Whispering to the* JUDGES.]

Did you notice that the dead man did not forgive Sender?

JUDGES ONE AND TWO

[*In low, frightened tones.*]

Yes, we did.

RABBI SAMSON

Do you know the dead man did not accept the verdict?

JUDGES ONE AND TWO

Yes, we realized that.

RABBI SAMSON

He failed to say Amen to Rabbi Azrael's sentence
·—you felt that too, no doubt.

JUDGES ONE AND TWO

Yes, distinctly.

RABBI SAMSON

It is a very bad sign——

JUDGES ONE AND TWO

Extremely——

RABBI SAMSON

Rabbi Azrael is terribly agitated—look at him.
See how his hands are trembling. [*Pause.*]   We
have done our share—we can go now.

[*The* JUDGES *slip out unobtrusively, and* RABBI
SAMSON *prepares to follow them.*]

RABBI AZRAEL

Rabbi, please remain until the Dybbuk has been
cast out—I should like you to perform the wedding
ceremony. [RABBI SAMSON *sighs and sits down
again, with bowed head.   An oppressive pause.*]
God of the Heavens, marvelously strange are Thy
ways, and secret, yet the flame of Thy Divine Will
illuminates with its reflection the path I tread. Nor

shall I stray from that path forever, either to the right or to the left. [*He raises his head.*] Michoel, is everything prepared?

MICHOEL

Yes, Rabbi.

RABBI AZRAEL

Let the maiden be brought.

[*Enter* SENDER *and* FRADE *with* LEAH, *in her wedding-gown, a black cloak over her shoulders. They seat her on the sofa.* RABBI SAMSON *takes his place behind* RABBI AZRAEL.]

RABBI AZRAEL

Dybbuk, in the name of the Rabbi of this city, who is present, in the name of a holy community of Jews, in the name of the great Sanhedrin of Jerusalem, I, Azrael ben Hadassah, do for the last time command you to depart out of the body of the maiden Leah, daughter of Channah.

LEAH [DYBBUK]

[*Firmly.*]

I refuse!

RABBI AZRAEL

Michoel, call in people to witness the exorcism— bring the shrouds, the horns and the black candles. [MICHOEL *goes out and shortly returns with* FIFTEEN MEN, *among them the* MESSENGER. *The* *shrouds, trumpets and candles are brought.*] Bring out the *scrolls.* [MICHOEL *gives a scroll each to seven, and a trumpet each to seven others.*] Stubborn spirit—inasmuch as you have dared to oppose our power, we deliver you into the hands of the Higher Spirits which will pull you out by force. Blow Tekiah!*

[*The horns are blown.*]

LEAH [DYBBUK]
[*Leaves her seat and struggles violently as against invisible assailants.*]
Let me alone—you shall not pull me away—I won't go—I can't go——

RABBI AZRAEL
Since the Higher Spirits cannot overcome you, I surrender you to the Spirits of the Middle Plane, those which are neither good nor evil. I now invoke *their* power to drag you forth. Blow Shevarim.*
[*The horns are blown again.*]

LEAH [DYBBUK]
[*Her strength beginning to fail.*]
Woe is me! The powers of all the worlds are arrayed against me. Spirits of terror wrench me

* Certain notes sounded on the Shofer, the sacred ram's horn.

and tear me without mercy—the souls of the great and righteous too have arisen against me. The soul of my own father is with them—commanding me to go— But until the last spark of strength has gone from me, so long shall I withstand them and remain where I am.

RABBI AZRAEL

[*To himself.*]

It is clear that One of Great Power stands beside him. [*Pause.*] Michoel, put away the scrolls. [MICHOEL *does so.*] Hang a black curtain over the altar. [*This is done.*] Light the black candles. [*This, too, is done.*] Let everyone now put on a shroud. [*All, including the two* RABBIS, *do so.* RABBI AZRAEL *stands with both arms upraised, an awe-inspiring figure.*] Rise up, O Lord, and let Thine enemies be scattered before Thee; as smoke is dispersed so let them be scattered. . . . Sinful and obstinate soul, with the power of Almighty God and with the sanction of the holy Scriptures, I, Azrael ben Hadassah, do with these words rend asunder every cord that binds you to the world of living creatures and to the body and soul of the maiden, Leah, Daughter of Channah. . . .

LEAH [DYBBUK]

[*Shrieking.*]

Ah! I am lost!

RABBI AZRAEL

. . . And do pronounce you ex-communicated from all Israel. Blow Teruah.*

MESSENGER

The last spark has been swallowed up into the flame.

LEAH [DYBBUK]

[*Defeated.*]
Alas!—I can fight no more. . . .
[*They begin to sound the horns.*]

RABBI AZRAEL

[*Hastily raising his hand to silence the horns.*]
Do you submit?

LEAH [DYBBUK]

[*In a dead voice.*]
I submit——

RABBI AZRAEL

Do you promise to depart of your own free will, from the body of the maiden, Leah, daughter of Channah, and never return?

LEAH [DYBBUK]

[*As before.*]
I promise——

* Certain notes sounded on the Shofer, the sacred ram's horn.

RABBI AZRAEL

Dybbuk—by the same power and sanction which deputed me to place you under the ban of anathema, I now lift from you that ban. [*To* MICHOEL.] Put out the candles—take down the black curtain. [MICHOEL *does so.*] Put away the horns. [MICHOEL *collects them.*] And dismiss the people— let them take off their shrouds before they go. [*Exeunt the* FOURTEEN *with* MESSENGER *and* MICHOEL.] [RABBI AZRAEL *prays with upraised arms.*] Lord of the world, God of charity and mercy, look down upon the suffering of this homeless, tortured soul which the errors and misdeeds of others caused to stray into the bypaths. Regard not its wrongdoing, O Lord, but let the memory of its virtuous past and its present bitter torment and the merits of its forefathers rise like a soft, obscuring mist before Thy sight. Lord of the world— do Thou free its path of evil spirits, and admit it to everlasting peace within Thy mansions. Amen.

ALL

Amen.

LEAH [DYBBUK]
[*Trembling violently.*]

Say Kadish * for me! The hour of my going was predestined—and it has come!

* The prayer for the dead.

RABBI AZRAEL

Sender, say Kadish.

[SENDER *begins the prayer as the clock strikes twelve.*]

SENDER

Yisgadaal—ve yiskadesh—shmeh raboh!*

LEAH [DYBBUK]

[*Springs up.*]

Aie!

[*Falls swooning upon the sofa.*]

RABBI AZRAEL

Bring the bride to the wedding canopy.

MICHOEL

[*Rushing in, greatly agitated.*]

The last rider has just come back. He says a wheel has come off the wagon so that the bridegroom and his party must walk the rest of the way. But they are at the hill, so they will be here soon—they've been sighted already.

RABBI AZRAEL

[*Profoundly astonished.*]

What was to be, shall be. [*To* SENDER.] Let the old woman remain here with the bride. We will go—all of us—to meet the bridegroom.

*Magnified and sanctified be His mighty Name!

[*He traces a circle round* LEAH, *from left to
right, takes off his shroud, which he hangs up
near the door, and goes out carrying his staff.*
SENDER *and* MICHOEL *follow him.*]
[*A long pause.*]

LEAH
[*Waking—in a faint voice.*]
Who is here with me? Granny—is that you?
Oh! I feel so strange, Granny—so weary. Rock
me in your arms.

FRADE
[*Caressing her.*]
No, little daughter—you mustn't feel that way..
My little child must not be sad. Let the Black Cat
be sad. My little one's heart must be as light as
down, as light as a breath, as white as a snowflake.
Holy angels should embrace her with their wings.
[WEDDING MUSIC *is heard.*]

LEAH
[*Frightened and trembling, seizes* FRADE'S *hand
for protection.*]
Listen! They are beginning to dance round the
holy grave to cheer up the dead bride and bridegroom.

FRADE
Be calm, my darling. No harm can come to you
now—a mighty power is standing guard over you

on every side.   Sixty giants, with drawn swords,
protect you from evil encounter.   The holy fathers
and holy mothers ward off the evil eye.

[*Little by little she drifts into a chant.*]

Soon they'll lead you under the canopy—
A blessed hour—a happy hour—
Comes your mother—the good and virtuous—
From the Garden of Eden—the Garden of Eden.
Of gold and silver are her robes.

Angels twain go out to meet her, go out to meet
        her—
Take her hands—one the right hand, one the left
        hand.
"Channele—Channele mine,
Why do you come decked out so fine?"

So Channele answers the angel:

"Why should I not come robed in state?
Is this not a day of days?
For my bright crown, my only daughter,
Goes to her wedding and luck goes with her."

"Channele, as in robes of state you go,
Why is your face all wan and pale with woe?"

So Channele answers the angel:

"What should I do but sorrow, on this day that my
    daughter's a bride,
For she's led to her wedding by strangers, while I
    must stand mourning aside?"

Under the canopy stands the bride, and old and
young bring her their greetings and good wishes.

And there stands the Prophet Elijah,
The great goblet of wine in his hand,
And the words of his holy blessing
Roll echoing over the land.

    [FRADE *falls asleep. Long pause.*]

LEAH

[*Her eyes closed, sighs deeply—then wakes.*]
Who sighed so deeply?

VOICE OF CHANNON

I.

LEAH

I hear your voice, but I cannot see you.

VOICE OF CHANNON

Because you are within a magic circle which I
may not enter.

LEAH

Your voice is as sweet as the lament of violins in
the quiet night. Who are you? Tell me.

VOICE OF CHANNON

I have forgotten. I have no remembrance of my-self but in your thoughts of me.

LEAH

I remember—now—the star that drew my heart towards its light—the tears that I have shed in the still midnight—the one who stood before me ever—in my dreams—was it you?

VOICE OF CHANNON

I——

LEAH

I remember—your hair, so soft and damp as if with tears—your sad and gentle eyes—your hands with the thin tapering fingers. Waking and sleeping I had no thought but of you. [*Pause—sadly.*] You went away and darkness fell upon me—my soul withered in loneliness like the soul of a widow left desolate—the stranger came—and then—then you returned, and the dead heart wakened to life again, and out of sorrow joy blossomed like a flower. . . . Why have you now once more forsaken me?

VOICE OF CHANNON

I broke down the barriers between us—I crossed the plains of death—I defied every law of past and present time and all the ages. . . . I strove against the strong and mighty and against those who know no mercy. And as my last spark of strength left me, I left your body to return to your soul.

LEAH

[*Tenderly.*]
Come back to me, my bridegroom—my husband—
I will carry you, dead, in my heart—and in our dreams at night we shall rock to sleep our little children who will never be born. . . . [*Weeps.*] And sew them little clothes, and sing them lullabies——
[*Sings, weeping.*]

> Hush—hush, little children—
> No cradle shall hold you—
> In no clothes can we fold you.

> Dead, that the living cannot mourn;
> Untimely lost and never born. . . .
> [*The Music of a wedding-march is heard approaching.*]

LEAH

[*Trembling.*]
They are coming to take me to a stranger under the canopy—come to me, my true bridegroom; come to me.

VOICE OF CHANNON
I have left your body—I will come to your soul.
[*He appears against the wall, white-robed.*]

LEAH

[*With joy.*]
Come, my bridegroom.　The barrier between us
is no more.　I see you.　Come to me. . . .

VOICE OF CHANNON

[*Echo.*]
Come to me.

LEAH

[*Crying out with joy.*]
I am coming. . . .

VOICE OF CHANNON

[*Echo.*]
And I to you. . . .
　　[VOICES *outside.*]

VOICES

Lead the bride to the canopy.
　[*Wedding-march is heard.* LEAH *rises, drop-
　ping, as she does so, her black cloak onto the
　sofa, and in her white wedding dress, to
　the strains of the music, she goes towards*
　CHANNON, *and at the spot where he has ap-
　peared their two forms merge into one.*]
　[RABBI AZRAEL *enters, carrying his staff, fol-
　lowed by the* MESSENGER. *They stand on the
　threshold. Behind them,* SENDER, FRADE *and
　the rest.*]

LEAH

[*In a far-away voice.*]

A great light flows about me . . . predestined bridegroom, I am united to you forever. Now we soar upward together higher and higher. . . .

[*The stage grows darker.*]

RABBI AZRAEL

[*With lowered head.*]

Too late!

MESSENGER

Blessed be a righteous judge.

[*It is now completely dark. As if from a great distance, singing is heard, scarcely audible.*]

Why, from highest height,
To deepest depth below,
Has the soul fallen?
Within itself, the Fall
Contains the Resurrection.

FINIS